THE HEART & SOUL OF KERRY FOOTBALL

Weeshie Fogarty played Gaelic football for Kerry at minor, under-21, junior and senior levels and won four senior county championship medals with East Kerry. He served as a national referee for fifteen years, played basketball for his county and with his club Killarney Legion, and has worked in every capacity as a player and an official.

He began his career as a psychiatric nurse in St Finan's Hospital, Killarney in 1962, when over 1,000 patients were locked up there. This is his third publication, following his book on legendary Kerry trainer Dr Eamonn O'Sullivan (*A Man Before His Time*) and his 2012 autobiography *Chasing the Kerry Dream: My Beautiful Obsession*.

Weeshie is a presenter and analyst with Radio Kerry; his sports programme *Terrace Talk* has won numerous National PPI and McNamee Awards. In 2015 he received the GAA's highest honour when he was presented with the McNamee Hall of Fame Award in Croke Park.

THE HEART & SOUL OF KERRY FOOTBALL

WEESHIE FOGARTY

THE O'BRIEN PRESS
DUBLIN

First published 2016 by
The O'Brien Press Ltd,
12 Terenure Road East, Rathgar,
Dublin 6, D06 HD27 Ireland.
Tel: +353 1 4923333; Fax: +353 1 4922777
E-mail: books@obrien.ie.
Website: www.obrien.ie

The O'Brien Press is a member of Publishing Ireland.

ISBN: 978-1-84717-827-5

1 3 5 7 8 6 4 2

16 18 20 19 17

Printed and bound by ScandBook AB, Sweden
The paper in this book is produced using pulp from managed forests

To my wife Joan,

daughters Denise and Carol Ann, son Kieran,

grand-daughters Lucy and Eva,

sister Sheila who emigrated to Birmingham in the fifties,

and in loving memory of my late family:

Mam and Dad,

brothers Dermie, Jimmy and Genie, and beautiful sister Kathleen Ann.

CONTENTS

FOREWORD 9

PREFACE 13

INTRODUCTION 17

1. FIRST FOOTBALL 29

2. LOW TIMES 36

3. THE CHALLENGE OF THE NORTHERNERS: COUNTY DOWN 49

4. PLAYERS ON STRIKE! 58

5. SLOW CHANGE 65

6. THE GOLDEN AGE: MICK O'DWYER 71

7. BEHIND CLOSED DOORS 94

8. KERRY'S GREATEST RIVALS 103

9. KERRY CAPTAINS: THE AGONY AND THE ECSTASY 125

10. KERRY WOMEN: BREAKING NEW GROUND 160

11. THE LADY FOOTBALLERS 179

12. MY ALL-TIME MOST SKILFUL/CLASSY/STYLISH KERRY FIFTEEN 188

13. REMEMBERING KERRY LEGENDS 218

14. KERRY SUPPORTERS: A DIFFERENT BREED 221

EPILOGUE: MEMORIALS 226

INDEX OF NAMES 231

FOREWORD

Weeshie Fogarty is the voice of Kerry football. He is known as no more than 'Weeshie'. The surest sign of affection and respect is when Kerry people drop your last name, because, well, you are one of a kind.

So where did it come from then, this lifelong love affair with Kerry football?

Boy and man, Weeshie has been there for his team and his people. Picture the scene sixty-three years ago in the Monastery National School in Killarney. There's a young boy in short pants waiting for the Sam Maguire. As is often said by his co-commentators on Radio Kerry: over to you, Weeshie.

And he writes so well. 'It [Sam] was lifted high in the air by the three Killarney men who had played the previous Sunday: Jackie Lyne, Tadhgie Lyne and Donie Murphy. A loud roar rent the air, followed by shrill whistling, cheering, shouting and stamping.'

The young Weeshie was hooked. Indeed, he went on to wear the green and gold himself, and this is the dream of nearly every Kerry child.

Weeshie was even brave enough to don the black, and refereed for many years with great distinction, rising to inter-county standard. Very, very few have worn the green and gold and the ref's black garb. Weeshie wanted to give something back to the game he loved so well, and he has kept on giving ever since that day when he first caught sight of Sam back in 1953.

Weeshie became a full-time commentator and journalist relatively late in life when he retired from his job as a psychiatric nurse in St Finan's Hospital in Killarney. The work had been tough and often heartbreaking. Weeshie met people at their lowest, and those years spent helping his patients to find their voices helped him to find his voice.

There's empathy and kindness there in abundance, and maybe that's why we listen to him on Radio Kerry and read his weekly columns in the *Kerryman*. The man who took up his new career just as his old job was folding has won several McNamee Awards for his services to GAA broadcasting. Weeshie has been so successful because he was a natural and he stayed natural.

His stories keep Kerry emigrants in touch with their own place. There's the one about the man who worked on gas pipelines in the freezing cold of Alaska, and it was Weeshie who kept him going with his stories from home.

Just a few months ago in New York I met a man who hadn't taken a drink for a good few years. He found it tough going, and when he heard Weeshie's voice traveling over the Atlantic, bouncing off satellites, all the way from Kerry, the tears came. Weeshie had been incredibly kind to him when he was battling with alcohol addiction in St Finan's.

When I was reading this book I could hear Weeshie's dulcet tones in my mind. The Killarney man writes as he speaks, and he speaks in the language of his own people. This is a talking book.

Maybe we could call that Killarney accent a sing-song voice. In the best possible sense. There's an internal melody for sure that rises and falls in tune with the ebb and flow of the game. He's a showman too. There are times when Kerry score a goal and you'd swear you were listening a South American soccer commentator screaming 'Gooooooooooooooal!'

He has this way of interviewing that gets you to talk openly about yourself and your times. It's a sort of a lulling of the interviewee into a true sense of security. Maybe he learned this skill from his days in St Finan's when men and women needed so badly to talk about their troubles.

We were doing a programme for Radio Kerry in the build-up to the 2005 All-Ireland Senior Football Championship final between Kerry and Tyrone. Weeshie took his shoes off and placed his feet up on the broadcast desk in the Radio Kerry studios in Killarney. We were drinking tea and chatting away. 'When will we start the interview?' I asked after 10 minutes or so, anxious to get home to work in the pub.

'Oh jay Billy, we've been on live for ages' came the reply from Weeshie as he dunked another biscuit in his tea.

Weeshie is modest and hard-working, and always on the look-out for a story. He feels a sense of duty to record the events of his time and the people who populated those events. There's the memory of that first trip to Croke Park when he saw Kerry beat Dublin in 1955. The true sign of top-class sports writing is when you wish you were there with the writer.

But if it is a love affair, well then it's tough love. Weeshie is not afraid to take on a controversial topic and he tells stories of secret strikes and the constructive dismissal of his boss in St Finan's. Dr Eamonn O'Sullivan, one of Kerry's most famous trainers, wasn't happy with the way the Kerry players were being treated when it came to expenses and feeding. He was eased out.

There's football gossip too.

He tells us of how Mick O'Dwyer and Mickey Ned O'Sullivan drove off home to Waterville rather than face doing an exam under Kevin Heffernan after a seminar on coaching. There's the story of how Micko went to Matt Busby for advice on coaching methods, and much, much more.

Weeshie does not go out of his way to stir up controversy or trouble. He does acknowledge that Kerry supporters are a hard enough bunch to satisfy. Weeshie only takes on a cause when he sees the need of affirmative action for the good of Kerry football. Not an easy thing to do in a small county where you're either a friend of someone or a friend of someone's friend. In Kerry there are zero degrees of separation.

I've often noticed people coming up to talk to Weeshie as if they've known him for year,s when in fact it's the first time they have ever really met up. He is himself, whether writing here in this book or in the paper or when he's high up in his commentary position.

Weeshie would talk football with anyone and everyone, all day and all night.

Sometimes he forgets where he is and what he's doing when the games get exciting. It's as if he's down there with us, cheering on his team. We know he is a real person with green and gold blood coursing through his veins.

He is as mad about the game of Gaelic football as he ever was. Weeshie Fogarty is still the small boy waiting for Sam in the Monastery School back in 1953.

Billy Keane, 2016

PREFACE

The idea for this publication was born in Cork in October 2014 – in beautiful Innishannon, to be precise. The wonderful Alice Taylor, author extraordinaire and a great friend, had asked me to speak at the launch of her latest book, *Do You Remember?*, at the Private Collector Gallery in the village. As I was chatting afterwards to the genial Michael O'Brien of The O'Brien Press, the discussion turned to Kerry football and its greatness, its secret and its people. To make the long story short, as they say, before the evening drew to a close Michael had persuaded me to consider writing about some of my experiences, and the idea for *The Heart & Soul of Kerry Football* was conceived.

Of course it's utterly impossible to capture the true soul of the Kingdom in print, but this is my honest endeavour to portray some of my experiences from 1955 to the present day: events, memories (good and bad), and the amazing players, officials and supporters who have contributed to the heart and soul of Kerry football.

Distance lends enchantment to the view, they say, and players and games back in the fifties and sixties may appear better in my recollections than they really were. But thankfully the youthful impressions remain fresh and vibrant: warming the heart, touching the very soul.

This book is a mere snapshot in time of the never-ending Kerry story. At some future date a far more competent hand than mine may add more chapters and further chronicle the achievements of Kerry footballers – men and women. The story to the present day is a fascinating one and, as I have observed on my travels, has brought great joy to thousands of Kerry exiles, particularly in America.

So what form will they take, those further chapters in Kerry's football story? The material will be supplied by the present generation of brilliant young footballers or those yet unborn. As in the past they will find great inspiration and ample incentive to follow in the footsteps of the legendary men who have gone before. What other county can boast of such a glorious tradition? Kerry must never forget. If you forget your past you have no present, and if you have no present how can you have a future?

My sincere thanks to Michael O'Brien and his helpful and patient team at The O'Brien Press. They all in their own hugely professional way helped me, encouraged me and challenged me along the way towards that final chapter. To Ide ni Laoghaire, Emma Byrne, Nicola Reddy and Brendan O'Brien, my sincere thanks for your wonderful courtesy and expertise as I struggled to complete the task. Failure was never an option with you beside me.

In my travels around Kerry and Ireland and beyond, pursuing my Radio Kerry duties, I have always had huge admiration for the work of our amazingly talented and professional photographers. I am so fortunate to have befriended them. They are a remarkable group of Kerry men and women and their work has been recognised and honoured in Ireland and beyond.

Shortly before his death on 21 May 2011, aged eighty-two, I spent an unforgettable afternoon at his West Kerry home with Pádraig Kennelly, photojournalist and founder of *Kerry's Eye*: one of my all-time favourite people. During a lengthy interview for my Radio Kerry *In Conversation* programme, I asked him why we were blessed in Kerry with so many people who excel in sports and life photography. His answer remains etched in my memory as if we had spoken only yesterday.

> I have no doubt, Weeshie, but that we are hugely influenced by the sheer beauty of our county: its towering mountains, its lakes and valleys, the mighty Atlantic pounding at our doorsteps; its flora and fauna; its poets, artists and authors; and of course its brilliant sportsmen and women and in particular its footballers, who have been part and parcel of the lives of practically every family in Kerry since 1884. Football and its heroes have shaped the way we approach our work.

And so I feel greatly privileged and indeed humbled to include in this book the work of fourteen of Kerry's gifted photographers. When asked, each without a moment's hesitation offered what they considered one of their favourite Kerry football photographs. They have helped greatly in my attempt to capture the heart and soul of Kerry football. It's a priceless collection within one publication.

My sincere thanks to Valerie O'Sullivan, Michelle Cooper Galvin, Don MacMonagle, Eamonn Keogh, Mike Brosnan, Domnick Walsh, John Stack, Christy Riordan, Kevin Coleman, Kerry Kennelly, Stephen McCarthy, Brendan Landy, John Reidy and Bryan O'Brien. Thanks too to the legendary GAA photographer Ray McManus and his Sportsfile team for providing photographs.

Brendan O'Sullivan, a Dublin man with Kerry roots and a passionate interest in Kerry football, contributes regularly to my award-winning Radio Kerry *Terrace Talk* programme, and has been a great help with some of my research for the book: thank you, Brendan. The content is based on my personal experiences since around 1955, but without the huge volume of interviews I have amassed over the years with all the great Kerry players, officials and supporters the work could not have been completed.

My position as presenter, analyst and interviewer with Radio Kerry for close to twenty years has provided me with a wonderful opportunity to record hundreds of interviews and has opened doors to people and places that would otherwise have been closed. With an amazing dedicated team of workers, Radio Kerry first went on air in 1990. To Paul Byrne, CEO, Fiona Stack, General Manager and Joe O'Mahony, Head of Sport (whose late father Seamus began my radio career) and to all the staff, my grateful thanks for such a life-changing opportunity. As my late dear mother always said to us, 'The Lord certainly works in strange ways.'

Weeshie Fogarty, 2016

INTRODUCTION

You asked what's the secret of Kerry and often I wished that I knew,
'Twill doubtless seem odd, though born on the sod, that question has puzzled me too.
You see the lad work in the meadow as he tosses the hay without rest,
And longs for the lengthening shadow as the sun slowly moves towards the West.
Then he'll hark to the thud of a football and things more important must yield,
For nothing must stay in a Kerry lad's way when the ball bounces high on the field.

These beautiful, evocative lines from the poem 'The Secret of Kerry', by Valentia man Joseph G. Smyth, underline the mystery, magic, spirit and traditions that abound in Kerry football. I first heard these words many years ago and they remain etched in my memory to this day. So powerful is their message that I have recited them at GAA gatherings all over the world.

From the beginning, let me emphasise that it is impossible to capture definitively in print the true meaning, spirit, uniqueness and secret of Kerry football. The man or women capable of accomplishing this has yet to be born. The truth is that the magic of Kerry's affair with the round ball is mystical, inexpressible, indefinable and invisible to the human eye. However, I will, like the poem 'The Secret of Kerry', do my best.

Let me take you back to 1953, the year that Kerry beat Armagh in the All-Ireland final. The county had been starved of success since 1946. As is traditional in the Kingdom, the cup was brought to all the schools in the county in the following weeks, including the Monastery national school in Killarney where I sat in one of the old wooden desks on the Tuesday after the match.

Brothers Emanuel and Philip were in a state of high anticipation as they waited for the great moment. Suddenly the door to the classroom opened wide and I saw, for the first time, this magnificent symbol of the GAA: the Sam Maguire Cup, gleaming brightly in the rays of September sun streaming in through the high classroom windows. It was lifted high in the air by the three Killarney men who had played the previous Sunday: Jackie Lyne, Tadhgie Lyne and Donie Murphy.

A loud roar rent the air, followed by shrill whistling, cheering, shouting and stamping of feet from the 100 or more boys gathered in the classroom. To me, the three players were giants, and the cup was mesmerising. There was something overwhelming about the moment – the handing down of tradition, the magic of Kerry, our birthright displayed before our very eyes.

Brother Philip then called for silence. After welcoming the three heroes, he stood at the top of the class, in front of the blackboard, and recited in perfect diction 'The Secret of Kerry'. Ever since, it has been for me the most significant, poignant and evocative of all Kerry poems.

After the mandatory half-day off from school was granted, and with no lessons that night, we rushed home to our parents, our heads spinning with the enormity of it all. Like every boy that day, I was captivated, consumed, smitten. The seeds had been set, and a lifetime of total involvement and commitment had begun.

So what's it like to grow up in Kerry immersed in the legendary stories and great deeds of iconic footballers? What's it like listening to great moments being recalled, time and time again, as they are passed down from generation to generation? Well, I can tell you, if you are born into a GAA family or become obsessed by the game through playing it with young friends, as I was, then it can become like an addiction, dominate your thinking, consume huge parts of your life and, for some, become more important than religion.

I know of one lifelong Kerry follower who died recently after leaving strict written instructions that a beautiful Kerry poem was to be recited at his funeral – nothing else, just the time-honoured 'Ghost Train to Croke Park'. This man had travelled to All-Ireland finals in the 1940s and '50s on the legendary 'ghost train' that steamed out of Killarney at midnight on the night before the match. It was the memory he cherished most as he lay on his death-bed. A Kerry follower in life and in death!

Kerry football is responsible for broken marriages, cancelled engagements, family feuds, weeks of celebration, and even more drunken weekends as those celebrations continue following local or county team victories. Defeats are followed by prolonged inquests, debate and questions in relation to selectors, players and the county board. Boys and girls are named after legends of the game. One father told me that when his young son was put to bed at night a football was laid on the pillow beside him. He explained the logic behind the move: 'When he opens his eyes in the morning the first thing he sees and smells is a football.' The young lad went on to play for the Kerry minors and under-21s.

I find it fascinating to observe the change that comes over the whole county every time Kerry reaches the All-Ireland final. The wonderful John B. Keane summed this up beautifully for me when he declared: 'A kind of a gossamer lunacy comes over Kerry people in the run-up to the final. Young and old, men and women lose all sense of themselves. It's football for breakfast, dinner and supper and everyone becomes an expert on the game.'

Jimmy Deenihan, politician and five-time All-Ireland winner, remarked to me once that Kerry football is also about art: 'Art and Gaelic football have long been aligned in Kerry. Visual and performing artists, writers and musicians have so often taken inspiration from the great Kerry players.' In Kerry, football is recognised as an art form as much as a sport.

And, yes, it is true that Kerry people book their holidays to coincide with the September showcase. Perhaps because of my job as presenter and analyst with Radio Kerry, I get requests from far and wide for the date of the final, as supporters at home and abroad plan for their traditional trip to Dublin. Munster finals, All-Ireland semi-finals, league finals are taken with a grain of salt; all eyes are on the biggest prize of all, the All-Ireland title.

Kerry supporters can also be highly critical of their teams, win or lose, and their great knowledge of the game is unrivalled. It is fair to say that most Kerry men and women have a vast knowledge of football and if, as often happens, I fall into their company in a pub or enter into conversation with supporters, I never cease to be amazed by what I learn. This, of course, is to be expected as the county has contested more All-Ireland finals, at all levels, than any other in the country.

Kerry footballers, past and present, are also great talkers about the game, and no matter where you go in the county you will bump into a player who has won All-Ireland medals at some level. One venue where you can meet them is a public house situated in College Street, Killarney, which until recently was owned by Jimmy O'Brien. It was, and still is, painted green and gold, the Kerry colours. Jimmy, the genial landlord, and his son Jim Bob had plied their trade in the pub since the 1950s, when Jimmy returned from America. It is one of the great GAA watering holes in the county. I consider it my local, and it is here, in this quaint, old-fashioned establishment, with its walls adorned with an array of ageing, fading football photographs and memorabilia, that you come near to capturing the real spirit and secret of Kerry.

Tom Long, one of the county's greatest from the 1950s and '60s, together with Donie O'Sullivan, the 1970 winning captain, 1984 winning captain Ambrose O'Donovan, Colm 'Gooch' Cooper and many more, stroll in and out for a drink or a chat as if they had never won that elusive Celtic cross. That's a feature of Kerry football – players will never get too big for their boots no matter how successful they become. Their accessibility is yet another reason why younger generations strive to follow in their footsteps.

Big match days, especially Munster finals against Cork played in Killarney's Fitzgerald Stadium, will entice a huge influx of supporters from both counties to this watering hole. It was always a first stop for Cork greats like Billy Morgan, Denis Allen, Jimmy Barry-Murphy, Con Paddy O'Sullivan and many more. Fall into company with any of those great players and you will be astounded at what you learn about the game. This is another part of the handing down of tradition, the process of learning and understanding the secrets of football.

No matter where you travel, a fierce pride, passion and deep understanding of Kerry football always comes shining through. In my travels abroad I have discovered that Kerry football means even more to those who have emigrated. It is their greatest connection to home. Never was this more evident than in 2015 when I spent a week in Boston. My generous hosts were Connie and Dolly Kelly, who live in the suburb of Belmont. Connie emigrated there in the 1960s and his deep love for Kerry football is astonishing. Now in his seventies, he has a wardrobe full of Kerry jerseys and, whatever function he attends – be it a birth, marriage or death – he is clad in his green and gold. I attended mass with him during my visit, and there he was collecting in the church with his basket while proudly wearing the Kerry jersey! Connie typifies for me what Kerry football means to our emigrants all over the world.

There's also Mickey Moynihan, who left his native Rathmore in the 1950s and whose life in New York has been centred around Kerry football. Willie Joe Casey lives in Chicago; he, his wife and their family have played a huge part in bringing to fruition the magnificent GAA complex, Gaelic Park, in the Windy City. For all of them, Kerry football is the single most important element in their lives. I found the same in Perth, Australia, when I made an unforgettable visit there in 1970.

In my travels for Radio Kerry, I have come across many other displays of what the spirit of Kerry football means to our emigrants. One man I met in a bar in the Bronx, New York, in 2015 informed me that he was on his way home to Kerry from Alaska, where he worked on the gas line in sub-zero temperatures, often dipping as low as –68°C. Kerry football was all he wanted to discuss, and he told me, 'I listened to you at last year's All-Ireland final on my laptop, in a small hut surrounded by Eskimos, who even got caught up in the excitement of it all. However, they had no idea what you were saying with that Kerry accent.'

Kerry football followers are a breed apart. Fanatical about the game, they expect and demand that their side win the All-Ireland every year. Nothing more, nothing less. The late, great Páidí Ó Sé, Kerry's legendary defender, once famously described them as 'animals' because they expect so much! Páidí tells a story about his late mother, Beatrice.

> When my nephews Darragh, Tomás and Marc were small, a visit next door to their grandmother was more or less a daily routine. It was football morning, noon and night in our home and the boys were literally brainwashed in relation to going on and playing with Kerry … My mother would arrange the three lads one behind the other in a straight line and she would then take the lead, a few well-chosen words such

> as 'By the left, quick march' and all four would set off around the tiny kitchen in perfect unison. They were marching (in their own minds) behind the Artane Boys' Band. It was wonderful to watch and of course that practice in the kitchen conducted by my mother stood the boys in good stead in later years.

Those three young boys, Páidí's nephews, would go on and march behind that famous band on many a historic day in Croke Park as they played major parts in helping Kerry to All-Ireland victory.

The Kerry feeling was expressed to me wonderfully by John Moriarty, the poet, author and philosopher, who was a passionate lover of Kerry and its footballers. On the week before Kerry's All-Ireland win over Mayo in 2006, on one of my frequent visits to his home, he described what a green and gold Kerry flag meant.

> You see, Weeshie, to your left you have the Punchbowl, and behind me is the Horses' Glen and Stumpa, and all the way over to East Kerry you have Cappagh, and in the far distance the Paps of Dana. We are surrounded by mountains here, and you have all the furze and the bracken and the dwarf furze growing around the house. Up here, in the nights, we hear the stags bellowing because the rut is on. It's magical. There are just a few families of us up here and we live in a small group of houses. It's a dead-end road, but right there, where no one but us will see it, is a lone Kerry flag. No member of the Kerry team will see it. There is no bus passing our door, no train, no cars, nothing.
>
> That flag, Weeshie, is celebrating the Kerry team and is in hope for the Kerry team. There are probably Kerry flags flying in secret places

> all over the county. It's almost like a Christmas candle lighting in the window of some house in some hidden place and no one will ever see it. But maybe only the angels will see it. It is there to tell the Kerry team that up here we have a flag flying for them, thanks to good old Mike Brosnan, who was a carpenter in his day: he erected the pole. This is our little community celebrating our beloved Kerry.

The ambition of every Kerry child is to wear the Kerry jersey at some level or grade, and in 1959 I had the privilege of achieving my dream when chosen in goal for the Kerry minors. It was a daunting experience. What remains with me is the pre-match talk given by the legendary Tralee man and passionate republican John Joe Sheehy, who was a selector on the day.

It is that sort of passion that has helped bring so much success over the years. County minor, under-21, junior and senior, schools, colleges, clubs and inter-firms, men and women, have all brought All-Ireland glory to Kerry since Tady Gorman led us to that historic first back in 1903. It's a remarkable achievement considering the size of the county, its location so far away from dense city populations and the vast number of miles travelled by players and supporters down through the decades.

On the other hand, the fact that Kerry is so remote and so close to the greatness of the Atlantic Ocean must have had a huge bearing on its development as the premier football county. The legendary *Kerryman* journalist Paddy Foley, following the 1937 replay against Cavan, summed up what this remoteness was all about from the perspective of the Kerry supporter:

> From poor homes on the fringes of the Atlantic came enthusiasts to travel by the ghost train from Tralee, Caherciveen and Killarney,

> then the night journey across country to Dublin, later the long weary wait until the game began. What other county has such a parallel to offer, the legendary train journey, the terrible inconvenience? Such is the atmosphere in which our All-Ireland boys are nurtured, the spirit which makes Kerry indomitable.

Former Kerry footballer and winning trainer Jackie Lyne had another take on our remoteness. He once remarked to me, when quizzed on the Kerry secret: 'With those bastards of mountains in front of us and those hoors of lakes behind us, sure there is nothing to do but play football.' I firmly believe that such harsh terrain has helped us produce those teak-tough, fearless men, in particular from West and South Kerry, seen in the great Kerry sides. These were men reared by the foaming Atlantic, whose high-fielding abilities – with no disrespect to other districts – have been vital to Kerry's success. They include Jerome O'Shea, Mick O'Dwyer, Mick O'Connell, Paddy Kennedy, Bill Casey, Jack O'Shea, Sean and Seamus Murphy, Páidí Ó Sé, Paddy Bawn Brosnan and, of course, the present generation of the outstanding Ó Sé brothers – Darragh, Tomás and Marc – and others too numerous to mention. North Kerry has gifted us with Tim Kennelly, Con Brosnan, Bob Stack, Eddie Dowling, Mick Finucane, Jack Walsh and Johnny Walsh.

These big, strong fielders of the ball allied to the cute, classy, nippy corner-forwards from the towns provide the perfect mix. The corner-forwards include players like Dick Fitzgerald, the Landers brothers, Tadhgie Lyne, Timmy O'Leary, Paudie Sheehy, Mikey Sheehy, Johnny Culloty, Garry McMahon, Derry O'Shea, Mick Gleeson, Ger Power, Maurice Fitzgerald and, of course, the most recent 'townie' stars Colm Cooper, James O'Donoghue and Mike Frank Russell.

And let's not forget the man from Sneem: the unluckiest captain of all, John Egan, whose dream of accepting the Sam Maguire Cup was destroyed by that Seamus Darby goal in 1982 when Offaly stole the chance of five-in-a-row. They are all men who perfected the art of corner-forward play; men with the grace, precision, craft, wonderful vision and deadly accuracy to get scores with the limited supply of ball that reaches their positions.

All great teams need leaders off the field, and here again Kerry have excelled. Examine closely any winning team from the county and it will have a manager/trainer or selectors on the line who themselves have achieved All-Ireland glory. This is one of the true secrets of the county – highly experienced men passing on their years of knowledge to the up-and-coming talent, handing down the traditions that they learned from the generation before them. It's fascinating to watch this unfold year after year. Past stars come and go, and fade into the background as a new man takes up the mantle.

Many may frown at the suggestion that tradition has something to do with the performances of our present-day teams, where everything is so high-tech and 'professional', but in my opinion the day we forget our past and the people who built the foundations of the GAA in Kerry is the day we begin to lose our true identify and fail to live up to the high standards that all other counties strive to emulate. While I might be in a minority of one on this, I firmly believe that the traditions I speak of are already being allowed to slip back into the mists of time, where they will be lost forever.

Early in 2003 I remarked to a prominent county board officer that it would be a big year as Kerry set out to win the All-Ireland, as, in doing so, we would be celebrating the centenary of the county's first win in 1903 and the jubilee win of 1953. I was quickly rebuked: 'Forget all that talk of the past; it has nothing to do with this year – we don't need to be putting extra pressure on the players.' As a result, there was no mention of commemorating those historic dates as the countdown to the final began. Tyrone beat Kerry, but maybe, if the significance of the year had been used as an extra motivating factor, the result would have been reversed against Mickey Harte's men.

Those charged with preserving and maintaining the great Kerry traditions would do well to remember that what was passed down from past generations is now their responsibility to cherish and nurture. Sadly, I fear that many of the present generation of officers pay little or no attention to this. Football fortunes and styles change constantly. The GAA and Croke Park are often now seen as money-making institutions, but I believe that to fail to preserve all those very special values that have been handed down to us would be a betrayal of those long since gone.

I will readily admit, however, that in this day and age, when all around us is changing, some of the traditions I cherish can at times have a damaging influence. Former Kerry footballer Dara Ó Cinnéide recently remarked:

> Tradition has a time and place in Kerry football. It can be a double-edged sword. Rather than being an inspiration to our All-Ireland win in 1997, which ended Kerry's eleven-year wait, the sheer weight of that tradition and the burden of expectation that came with it was too great for a lot of players. Even having Ogie Moran as manager – a living legend with eight All-Ireland medals – couldn't help.
>
> It was only when Páidí Ó Sé – another of the great generation – took over and told us to forget all the baggage of the past decade, and pay no heed to the voices from within the traditions of Kerry football, that players felt sufficiently liberated to go on and forge their identity.

Also, of course, in an era when football and the preparation process have reached a near-professional level, the notion that Kerry footballers have a divine right to win because of their DNA and traditions is simplistic. The game has changed massively, and in order to maintain that winning attitude, Kerry footballers have to work harder and harder. Maybe there is a constant play between the two attitudes: tradition sometimes has a quiet presence, a background existence; at other times it can be given a louder voice. Maybe the trick is to know when to give voice to it and when to let it be silent.

The county also needs to adapt – a fact understood by Eamonn Fitzmaurice, a man steeped in tradition who led the Kingdom to a completely unexpected All-Ireland win in 2014, his great-grandfather having won a hurling All-Ireland medal with Kerry in 1891. He realised that Kerry would have to adapt to new ways of winning matches, but knew the great well of tradition that is there to be drawn from. That tradition and the football knowledge of the men in charge will not win All-Irelands every year, but while most other counties struggle to be competitive on a regular basis, Kerry, with some notable exceptions, will always be competitive.

As I have witnessed down through the decades, counties such as Dublin, Down, Tyrone and Galway have defeated Kerry in finals, but Kerry has always adapted and changed to confront those new challenges, reflecting the way the game has been transformed over time. This, allied with the county's traditions, is the greatest 'secret' of all.

1

FIRST FOOTBALL

It's inevitable as night follows day that any young boy or girl born and bred in Kerry will at some stage of their early development be afforded the opportunity to kick a football and to dream of winning an All-Ireland medal with his county in Croke Park. I have found it fascinating during a lifetime of deep involvement to observe and wonder at the burning passion for Kerry football that dominates every town, parish and townland in the county. It supersedes practically everything else, and it lasts from the cradle to the grave.

After my son Kieran was born, a group of friends visited my wife Joan in the Killarney hospital. The first ever present the baby received was a football, which was placed at the bottom of his cot. The expected first big outing for every budding young Kerry footballer is a trip to Croke Park for some championship match, or to stand on the side of a street and dream as the Sam Maguire Cup is paraded through the county towns following All-Ireland victory. The visit of the cup to the schools around the county is just another method by which the youth are indoctrinated with dreams of emulating their heroes.

In September 1953 I was just eleven years old. The full-time whistle had just been blown in the All-Ireland final Croke Park, and Kerry had defeated Armagh in that historic encounter. We had listened to the match on an old

Bush radio outside McNeill's public house and sweet shop in Lower New Street. While Dr Eamonn O'Sullivan and his selectors had been laying their plans for the final in the weeks before the game, another group was also busy planning and plotting for what would be their own special All-Ireland. I refer to the many young boys of my age group who lived in this area of the town, just a stone's throw from the Killarney National Park. It was in that park that we spent our boyhood days. This was our playground: fishing for trout and eels in the river Denaght, snaring rabbits, climbing the towering trees, playing cowboys in the dense shrubbery and always being on the look-out for the estate gamekeeper. Long lazy summer days were spent swimming in the lakes. It was a magical time. Darkness would descend, the bonfire would be lit, a frying pan produced, and sausages and rashers stolen from home and secretly wrapped in swimming togs and towel behind our mothers' backs would be soon sizzling beautifully over the blazing fire. Then the All-Ireland finals that Kerry contested would be discussed at length.

Our imaginations were vividly captured in the run-up to the 1953 final. The *Kerryman* gave the match great coverage. A special supplement was produced; players were interviewed. Of course there was no television or local radio back then. The *Kerryman* was the bible of Kerry football and its GAA journalist Paddy Foley, who wrote under the initials PF, was one of the best in the country. For us Killarney boys, our heroes on that magnificent team were Jackie Lyne, Tadghie Lyne and Donie Murphy, all from the town.

Mulcahy's boot and shoe shop was at the top of our street. In the weeks preceding the final the shop windows were bedecked with green and gold flags, big pictures of the local players, old Blackthorn football boots and socks, and right in the centre was a silver cup which I later learned was the prize for the winners of the old Killarney Street League. Nestling on top of that cup was a beautiful white pigskin football with 'O'Neills' printed boldly in black lettering. It was the first time I had seen a pigskin football, and I was dazzled by it newness and whiteness. We would gather every day after school and gaze at the wonders in this window; most of all our eyes feasted on the football.

Danno Keeffe (not the legendary Kerry goalkeeper) was the man in charge of the sports section of the shop. In later life he and I became great friends as we were members of the Killarney Legion Club. Danno was a member of the Kerry junior football panel and played a few games with the seniors. He was one of the stars of the Kerry basketball team that won the county's first ever All-Ireland title in 1957. One day a few of us summoned up the courage to enter the shop and ask Danno the price of the football. 'Well boys,' he replied, 'it's five pounds, five shillings and sixpence, but if ye come in with the five pounds ye can have it, is that fair?'

We were determined to have that football and so we set about raising the money. Just outside the town on the Killorglin road was the Killarney dump, where all the town's refuse was disposed of. It covered a huge area, wide open to the elements, and the smell was horrible. But it was here that the secret of raising funds to purchase the ball lay. We became known as 'the New Street picaroons' as we began collecting jam jars from the dump. Every day after school in the Monastery we would gather at Christy Healy's shop on our street and run the two miles to the dump. With the seagulls and crows swooping and screeching over our heads in their fury at being disturbed, we scoured the vast area, ignoring the awful smell. My brother Genie had salvaged an old canvas potato bag from our father's shed, and this would be quickly filled with filthy two-pound jam jars.

Our next stop on the way home was the Denaght River, running parallel with the Port Road and just across from St Mary's Cathedral. Off with the shoes, into the river, and the washing and cleaning of the jam jars commenced. T.T. O'Connor's shop in High Street was the next stop; they had stores at the back where we sold the jars to the man in charge, two pennies for each jar. Donie O'Sullivan was appointed the keeper of the money, and it was an excited group of young picaroons who finally landed the five pounds on the counter to Danno. We watched in glorious anticipation as he retrieved the ball from the window. He then proceeded to pump it with a special valve attached to a bicycle pump and then, with deft, experienced fingers, he laced up the opening with a leather thong. The ball was ours. It was handed around from one to the other, and I will never forget the soft feel and beautiful leathery smell of that first ever football. Until then, Genie and I had made our own ball, a bundle of pages from the *Kerryman* or *Cork Examiner* tied together with some of my mother's knitting yarn.

During one of those days scavenging in the Killarney dump I uncovered a large, silver-plated oil lamp. I brought it home and watched, enthralled, as my mother cleaned and shone what was to be our very own Sam Maguire Cup. Plenty of elbow grease and a fair spread of Brasso transformed this dirty old lamp into a beautiful shining spectacle. And so that day in the dim and distant past, when the full-time whistle had sounded in Croke Park and Armagh had been defeated, a crowd of young New Street boys raced to the St Brendan's Seminary field situated in the New Road not far from our homes. And it was there in that field, now the site of Killarney Community College, that our All-Ireland final was played. Two teams of twelve battled it out until darkness descended. Michael Clifford was the winning captain and Brother Philip from our Monastery school, who had refereed the contest, presented the 'cup' to the captain.

* * *

My first big outing was, of course, to Croke Park for a final. I was fourteen years of age in 1955 when Kerry, captained by John Dowling, faced Dublin in the All-Ireland final. Some of my boyhood friends and I secured tickets from our club and headed for Dublin on the legendary 'ghost train' that left Killarney station at midnight the night before the match. It was an unforgettable experience. Killarney station was a heaving mass of humanity, all waiting to board the train.

Many of the Kerry supporters were in high spirits having spent the previous few hours in the local pubs: Teddy O'Connor's, The Park Place Hotel and Jack C. O'Shea's in High Street, Charlie Foley's on New Street, Christy McSweeney's, Jimmy O'Brien's, Murphy's and the Arbutus Hotel in College Street were big GAA gathering houses.

No flags, jerseys or banners were to be seen back then. The only Kerry colours available were the paper green and gold caps and maybe a tuppenny badge sold by Killarney town bell man, Pats Coffey. It was a common sight following a rainy match day to see supporters' faces streaked with the Kerry colours as the dye from those paper hats ran down their necks and faces. Practically all the men were dressed in their 'Sunday suits', shirts and ties. Jeans were not yet in vogue, and tracksuits tops and all the various Kerry GAA attire was a fashion for a future generation. The trains were usually packed. Each carriage would seat about ten people and I have vivid memories of seeing youngsters sound asleep on the baggage racks overhead.

As the old steam engine huffed and puffed out of the station the pack of cards would be produced, somebody's overcoat spread across the knees of the occupants would act as a table and a game of thirty-one would begin. All kinds of sandwiches, packed in shoe boxes, would appear as the miles sped by. Big lumps of pig's head and crubeens were highly popular, especially after the few pints of porter. I recall big Cidona flagon bottles being passed around – though now containing beautiful dark draught Guinness. The sound of music rose up as a box player warmed up and this would lift the spirits. By the time the train had left Mallow mighty sing-songs were to be heard all along the corridor of the train.

Towns and villages flashed by in the pitch darkness as the men and women from all corners of Kerry discussed the upcoming match. Just as today, all the great players of days gone by would be recalled with huge reverence. Great games, memorable scores, and tales of previous journeys helped shorten the trip. Hours into the journey, heads would begin to nod and loud snoring would reverberate around the carriages as everyone attempted to find the most comfortable position, which was not an easy task, and catch some sleep. And the train would stop for one reason or another at every station along the way!

Finally, around six in the morning Kingsbridge (Heuston) Station would be reached. First stop was some church along the Liffey quays for mass, where many a supporter could be seen fast asleep, and then a big breakfast in the first café found open for business. That day in 1955 we were queuing outside Croke Park by midday. A massive crowd of 87,102 watched spellbound as a completely unfancied Kerry defeated the so-called unbeatable Dublin machine, 0–12 to 1–6. I had seen my first final, and every minute of that wonderful day remains etched in my memory to this very day.

Four years later – 1959 – I attended my second All-Ireland final and was privileged to see Mick O'Connell captain Kerry to victory. The minor game, in which Dublin beat Cavan, made me think of what might have been. I had played in goal for the Kerry minors earlier that year, but Cork beat us in Killarney in the Munster final: my dream of playing in Croke Park with Kerry would have to wait for a few more years. Little did I realise as I watched this curtain-raiser that fifty years later I would become friendly with a member of that losing Cavan team. Kevin McCormack was, I recall, a lovely, nippy corner forward that day and caused the Dublin defence plenty of worry.

And now I fast-forward to my home town, Killarney, in the summer of 2011, and I fall into conversation with a street musician sitting on the sidewalk outside Reidy's century-old pub in Main Street. He is playing a variety of musical instruments, dressed in a vivid red jumpsuit and sporting a long, flowing, snow-white beard. He recognises my voice from my Radio Kerry sports programmes and football quickly becomes the main topic of conversation. I subsequently learn that he is the same Kevin McCormack whom I had seen play in Croke Park all those years ago. He had fallen into hard times, taken to the road and was one of the few remaining true street musical entertainers. We have since become great friends, and when the summer ends in Killarney, Kevin heads for Spain or some other sunny place where he can entertain and make a few pounds.

Kerry had an easy win in the senior final that day, defeating Galway 3–7 to 1–4. There were 85,897 supporters in attendance and Mick O'Dwyer won his first All-Ireland medal.

2

LOW TIMES

On the evening of Sunday, 2 June 1957, two old gentlemen were having their daily walk near the village of Glenbeigh in County Kerry. As they passed the house of a neighbour, the occupant, a passionate Kerry GAA follower, came rushing out to meet them. 'Did ye hear the news? Kerry were beaten by Waterford! Beaten by *Waterford!*' It was as if a national catastrophe had occurred. His two friends paused as the news began to sink in. They looked at each other with incredulity and one of them replied, 'Where did you hear that ridiculous story?'

'I just heard it on the evening sports news. And it was Michael O'Hehir who read out the score.'

Once again the two walkers looked at each other disbelievingly. Then one of them responded: 'O'Hehir was it that said that? I wouldn't believe one word he'd say. Sure, he was always against Kerry anyway.'

In Waterford that day most people had opted for beaches like Clonea, Ardmore and Tramore rather than the footballing venue of Walsh Park, where the entire country expected that Kerry would be going through the motions against Waterford in the first round of the Munster senior football championship. Waterford man Johnny Ryan, a great Kilrossanty servant, bumped into a close friend as he cycled home from the match. 'Did you hear the result from Walsh Park?' Johnny asked, adding, 'We beat Kerry by a point.' Like the men in Glenbeigh, Johnny's friend was disbelieving: 'Johnny, boy, go away, tell that to the marines and pull the wool over someone else's eyes.'

It was a result that sent shock waves through every county in the land: without doubt the greatest sensation in the history of the GAA, even to this day. That defeat by Waterford is still spoken about. It has entered the realm of folklore and many stories have built up over the years in relation to one of the blackest days in Kerry football history.

I was a teenager, but I can still vividly recall the sun-splashed Sunday in June when Waterford's Tom Cunningham kicked the point that ensured his sporting immortality in the dying seconds of a thriller. So, following the replay defeat to Cork the previous year and the late Niall Fitzgerald winning point, the euphoria of the '55 win over Dublin had well and truly evaporated in just two years. No one saw this sensational elimination of the Kingdom coming. How could Kerry have sunk so low?

In fact, 1957 had begun as a very promising year for the county. I attended my first ever National League final in Croke Park in May of that year as Kerry squared up to Galway: the 1955 All-Ireland champions against the 1956 League winners. Amazingly, Kerry had not contested a League final since 1931/32, when Miko Doyle captained them to victory. With five minutes left for play in that '57 final the teams were level at six points each. It was a memorable contest.

My eyes had been glued all day to the two most renowned footballers of that era: Galway's Frank Stockwell and Sean Purcell. Affectionately known as 'The Terrible Twins', they were at the height of their greatness at this time. Then it happened. I can still visualise it as if it were only yesterday. Purcell running out to the corner flag at the Canal end, selling dummies all over the place and centring to the Kerry goal mouth where Stockwell had glided into position. A flick of the right wrist and the ball was nestling in the Kerry net, giving 'Marcus' O'Neill no chance to save. The 'Twins' then added a point each and the Tribesmen ran out winners 1–8 to 0–6.

That defeated Kerry side of 1957: Donal 'Marcus' O'Neill, Jerome O'Shea (captain), Ned Roche, Tim 'Tiger' Lyons, Sean Murphy, John Dowling, Colm Kennelly, Denny O'Shea, Tom Long, Paudie Sheehy, Tom Moriarty, Tadghie Lyne, Tom Collins, Mick Murphy, Dan McAuliffe. Pop Fitzgerald came on for Tom Collins. Mick O'Connell was injured and missed the game. Peter McDermott, the renowned footballer from Meath, was the referee.

Kerry's football spirit had been dented, but when your county is losing in its favourite sport, the feeling that all is not lost can be encouraged by a completely different sporting success. In this case the spur of enthusiasm was provided by basketball. The Saturday evening before the League defeat a Kerry basketball side had written themselves into history's pages when they beat Antrim 34–31 to win the county's first ever All-Ireland title in Cathal Brugha Barracks, Dublin. Tadghie Lyne had helped Kerry to reach that final but missed the game due to the National League fixture. Members of the winning basketball side included Paddy Culligan, who later became Garda Commissioner and played inter-county football with Kerry and Cork; Danno Keeffe (Killarney) and Noel Dalton (Tralee) also played with the county footballers. The rest of the victorious basketball side were Paddy and Tadge O'Reilly, Denis Moriarty, Paul Cantillon (captain), Dominic Moriarty, Maurice Breen, Christy Walsh, Hal O'Donoghue. Denis Foley, who later entered Dáil Éireann, was the county secretary. So, long before Kieran Donaghy and Micheál Quirke, basketball played a big part in Kerry's sporting life.

Heading into the football championship in 1957 – the first step in the attempt to regain the Sam Maguire – Kerry and Galway were the bookies' favourites. Kerry had won five of the seven Munster titles that decade and had played in three All-Ireland finals, winning in '53 and '55, so the trip to Waterford seemed like a formality. Contrary to what we have been told, the team was reasonably prepared, having put in some training for the League final, and a challenge game against Cork in Mallow had unearthed fresh talent for the coming season. But, amazingly, even turning up in Waterford would prove to be a difficult task. Just a day before the game four Kerry players pulled out and the selectors were left with only fifteen fit players and one injured man, Dinny O'Shea.

Things went from bad to worse. The brilliant defender Sean Murphy had university exams and failed to travel too. Tom Moriarty also stayed at home, as did Jack Dowling. Then Kerry were left without a regular recognised goalkeeper when 'Marcus' O'Neill, the St Mary's Caherciveen man – in my view the best Kerry goalkeeper never to win an All-Ireland medal – also failed to travel. Now, 'Marcus' himself told me that 'I notified the Kerry selector Gerald O'Sullivan on the Friday before the game that I was not going to Waterford and they should pick up a goalkeeper in Tralee or Killarney, so it was the county board's own fault that they did not organise a replacement for me … I was made the scapegoat and blamed in the wrong for what transpired, and what about the other Kerry players that failed to travel?'

It was well known that problems had arisen in Caherciveen due to the captaincy of the Kerry team in that year. Some things never change in Kerry, and the question of who will be captain of the county team continues to this day to cause untold unrest at least once or twice a decade. The county board has in my opinion failed badly to step in and rectify this ongoing dilemma.

The situation is this. The Kerry county champions are entitled to the captaincy, and if a divisional team wins, the winning club team within that division nominates the captain. If a club side wins the county championship, that club nominates its preference. Generally it works out well, but recent and past events have left a sour taste in many mouths. It would be so simple to hand over the appointment of the captaincy to the manager of the team. Surely he would be competent to appoint the most deserving player for the job.

So here we were in '57. South Kerry were reigning county champions and Waterville were the club champions of that district. Mick O'Dwyer, a Waterville man, made his championship debut that day in Dungarvan but his club decided that he was not ready for the role of Kerry captain and they passed it over to St Mary's Caherciveen; the underlying problems then came to the surface. A meeting of the St Mary's club was called to sort out the appointment. They had three men on the Kerry panel: Ned Fitzgerald (father of Maurice), Jerome O'Shea and 'Marcus' O'Neill. Jerome O'Shea, the hero of the 1955 win over Dublin, had been captain the previous year. It appeared that the decision would rest between O'Neill and O'Shea. Legend has it that the goalkeeper refused to travel when he met up with the players in Caherciveen the Saturday before the match and was informed that the captain had been chosen.

Years later both men gave me their sides of the story. Jerome was adamant that he would have withdrawn from the contest except that a club delegation persuaded him to let his name go forward. I spoke to 'Marcus' in his son's home between Glenbeigh and Caherciveen one winter's day, and he too was adamant that he would have been happy to see either Mick O'Dwyer or Mick O'Connell lead the team out against Waterford. 'I felt the honour should be passed around; Jerome had been captain the year before so what was wrong with another man having the honour?', he concluded.

That St Mary's meeting finally decided that if selected Ned Fitzgerald would captain his county, which he did. They voted to have Jerome O'Shea as second choice. 'Marcus' did not enter the picture and finished well down the field when the votes were counted. He addressed the meeting and immediately walked out.

On the day of the match there was utter confusion in the Kerry dressing room before the game, and the filling of the goalkeeping position was comical to say the least. Corner-back 'Tiger' Lyons volunteered to play between the sticks; Tralee's Tim Barrett, who had played at corner-back in the heartbreaking All-Ireland minor final defeat to Dublin in 1954, was present as a spectator and would be drafted to play in Tim's usual position. However, on the way out onto the field Lyons changed his mind and decided that Barrett should be the goalie. It was really unbelievable stuff. To cap what is one of the most bizarre stories I have ever encountered in relation to Kerry football, it was decided to ask the reporter for the *Kerryman* newspaper – John Barrett, a useful club player – to tog out. John later worked for the *Irish Post* in London. Denny O'Shea was the only other sub available and he, one of the stars of the '55 win, was suffering from a serious ankle injury.

Events got even worse when it was discovered that Tom Collins had left his boots back at the hotel. The county secretary Tadge Crowley was dispatched to fetch them, and eventually the patched-up Kingdom were ready to begin. After half-time Kerry led comfortably by eight points. Then the drama began to unfold before the disbelieving Waterford supporters. And it was a Kerryman, a native of Kenmare, who initiated the downfall of his own county. George Whyte, who had played corner-forward for the Kerry minors in the 1954 minor defeat by Dublin, took a free for Waterford that Barrett let slip through his fingers into the net. Shortly after this the goalie was bundled over the line for another goal, and the sides were level. And then the unbelievable happened. Waterford's inter-county hurling star Tom Cunningham stormed up-field and from fifty yards out kicked what transpired to be the winning point. Paudie Sheehy had a last-minute chance to level but kicked wide from close in. Waterford had recorded a never-to-be-forgotten victory, 2–5 to 0–10. The Kerry team: Tim Barrett, Jerome O'Shea, Ned Roche, Tim 'Tiger' Lyons, Mick O'Dwyer, John Dowling, Michael Kerins, Tom Long, Mick O'Connell, Paudie Sheehy (0–1), Ned Fitzgerald (captain, 0–3), Tadghie Lyne (0–2), Pop Fitzgerald (0–1), Tom Collins (0–1), Dan McAuliffe (0–2). Sub: Denny O'Shea for Tom Collins. Other sub togged: John Barrett. Selectors: John Joe Sheehy, Gerald O'Sullivan, Jackie Lyne, Paddy 'Bawn' Brosnan, Fr Curtin. Trainer: Dr Eamonn O'Sullivan.

Kerry substitute John Barrett was scathing in his report for the *Kerryman* the following week, stating: 'Waterford were in fact a very poor team and would be far from a sensation even in junior ranks. However Kerry would have won comfortably had they rated their own ability a little less highly.' The headlines said it all: 'Over-confidence cost Kerry a sure victory.' Back then, as now, the referee came in for some stick. The appointed man, Sean Cleary of Clonmel – known as a very strict disciplinarian – withdrew, and Seamus Hayes from Tipperary, who was noted for not blowing the whistle too often, took over; this suited the more rugged Waterford men.

It was Waterford's first championship victory over their honour-laden opponents since 1911, and how they celebrated. One of Kerry's great GAA servants and now former chairman of the county board, Gerald McKenna, was working in Dublin in 1957. When he heard the result on the radio he simply could not believe it and rang the radio station to check it out. On the Thursday before the game, legend has it that Pat Fanning, who was then chairman of the Waterford county board and later became President of the association, entered Mickey Landers' pub in Dungarvan where the selectors were gathered in the back room. The table was littered with full and empty pint glasses of porter and the air was heavy with cigarette smoke. One of the selectors was scribbling down a list of names on a sheet of paper. Fanning was a lifelong member of the Pioneer Association; he told the selectors that never again was a Waterford football team to be picked in a public house and that they were bringing the name of the county into disrepute. He then left in disgust.

That Sunday afternoon following the final whistle, Pat entered the Waterford dressing room where supporters and players were cheering, hugging and dancing in total delight. The place was sheer bedlam. Fanning stood up on a small, rickety table, and when order was restored he shouted out to massive cheers and celebrations, 'Never again do I want to see a Waterford football team picked anywhere else but in the back room of Mickey Landers' pub!' Waterford went on to lose the Munster final to Cork 0–16 to 1–2, which proved that they were far from a good side.

Waterford's historic victory entered the folklore of Gaelic games in both counties. The stories surrounding that famous day have grown and developed down the years. We were always told that the taxi driver for some of the Kerry team was called to tog out, but, as I explained, that is not true. It was the *Kerryman* reporter. This sounds just as good.

Kerry were shattered. It is reported that the legendary Kerry footballer John Joe Sheehy, one of the selectors that day, was heard to say in the dressing room as he sat with his head in his hands, 'Oh my God, oh my God, we had better wait until darkness before we arrive back home to Kerry.' There were grave repercussions for 'Marcus' O'Neill at the following week's county board meeting. The South Kerry goalkeeper wrote a letter to the secretary of the board which contained some caustic comments about the whole affair, and a long debate took place on the rights and wrongs of all the players who did not travel to Waterford. Frank Sheehy chaired the meeting and contributors included Pat O'Meara (Killarney Legion), Micheál Ó Ruairc, John Joe Sheehy, Sean O'Donoghue (John Mitchels), Michael O'Loinsigh and Denny Kissane (South Kerry).

Most of the club delegates present did not take part in the debate. From attending county board meetings for over ten years, I know that it is usual not to get involved in something that does not involve your own club. Not a healthy democratic attitude, I believe. Selector John Joe Sheehy was furious with this silence, and he stood up and exclaimed, 'Is there anybody here to defend the selection committee? It's not for me to do so but this silence by the members is shameful, the silence is awful.'

Closing the debate, the chairman said, 'I thought the board's silence on the matter tonight was a very poor effort indeed.' The chairman then suspended O'Neill for six months under rule 41, from 2 January. It was decided to accept Sean Murphy's explanation that he was doing examinations and to defer the cases of Jack Dowling and any other player involved until their explanation arrived. Finally, it was stated that Tom Moriarty had written prior to the match stating that he had decided to retire from the game. The following year, 1958, 'Marcus' was back between the posts to help Kerry win the Munster championship. They defeated Tipperary and then Cork, but went under to Derry in the All-Ireland semi-final. He conceded just one goal – to Derry – during the three games.

Irrespective of what transpired before, during or after the game that Sunday afternoon in Dungarvan, one thing is certain. The Kerry fifteen that went out had a multitude of stars and All-Ireland medal holders on display. Mick O'Dwyer made his senior championship debut on that team while rising stars such as Mick O'Connell and Tom Long were also in the line-up. It appears to me that John Barrett got it spot-on when he reported that over-confidence and nothing else cost Kerry victory.

It was a harsh lesson for the county but has stood one and all in good stead, and praise must go to Waterford for the way they held out. Results like this make the association great.

For the Munster final Waterford had in their ranks another Kerry man. Micksie Palmer lived in Waterford but had missed the game against Kerry; he lined out at corner-back for Waterford against Cork. The Sneem man had won All-Ireland medals with Kerry in 1953 and 1955. To add a final twist to the tale, Jackie Lyne, who had been a selector when Kerry played Waterford, was appointed to referee that Munster final. It was the first and last Munster final he handled.

Kerry football reached an all-time low in the early and middle sixties. The county suffered humiliating defeats in the championship, going under to Down, Galway and twice to Cork. In 1962 an All-Ireland win over a very poor Roscommon had proved a false dawn. Still, that game was notable for two reasons. Firstly, Sean Óg Sheehy followed in the footsteps of his father John Joe in captaining his county to victory: a unique occurrence. Secondly, the fastest goal ever scored in an All-Ireland final to this day was recorded after just thirty-two seconds when Garry McMahon fisted to the Canal goal following a long free by Mick O'Connell. I became great friends with Garry, a wonderful composer and singer of Kerry football ballads, before he sadly died still a young man, and he loved telling the story of his yearly visit to the All-Ireland final. 'As the referee throws in the ball,' he'd recall, 'I'll look at my watch and when it passes the thirty-two second mark I'll turn to those seated alongside me and remark, my record is safe for another year.'

Many things about the game of Gaelic football were of a low standard in those years. The Munster final of 1962 was memorable for all the wrong reasons, and I will go as far as to say that it was one of the dirtiest inter-county games I have ever seen. The old Cork Athletic Grounds was a fairly intimidating place, and that day – 15 July 1962 – I was standing on the old grassy embankment. On the far side was the very dilapidated stand with its rusting galvanised roof. The game was an easy one for Kerry as they strolled to a 4–8 to 0–4 win. It was the Kingdom's fifth Munster crown in succession and was notable for the fact that Mick O'Connell scored his one and only championship goal for his county. It came late in the second half, when he soloed in from the wing and hit an angled shot high to the Cork net. He added a point from the kick-out to finish with 1–4 to his credit.

O'Connell's goal was overshadowed by some very unsavoury incidents both on and off the field. I have never before or since seen such naked aggression by fans as I saw that day. The game was very physical from the start and there were numerous off-the-ball incidents behind the referee's back. Punches were constantly being thrown by some players and elbows were flying in the tackles. Referee Moss Colbert of Limerick had a near-impossible task as he attempted to keep the game under control.

Then Cork star Eric Ryan was injured in a heavy collision and had to leave the field. As the game become more and more physical, sections of the crowd began booing and shouting at players and referee. Then all hell seemed to break loose. Kerry's centre-back Noel Lucy and Cork's Joe O'Sullivan were sent off. Now I had a perfect view of events as they unfolded off the field. As Lucy was walking along the sideline to the Kerry area, some supporters showered him with sods that they tore from the embankment. Kerry secretary Tadgh Crowley and Chairman Jim Brosnan was walking with the Kerry player and had to duck and dodge as the missiles rained down. The atmosphere was frightening and hostile.

Then from behind the goal to my right a section of the crowd began bombarding the Kerry goal with sods and stones. The two umpires at that goal left their positions and took shelter in the net with Kerry goalkeeper Johnny Culloty, who had not been involved in any incident. The situation looked as if it would get out of control. After the game a friend of mine told me that a young Cork 'supporter' picked up a bottle with the obvious intent of hurling it at a Kerry player. As he was about to throw the missile the Kerry man hit him a belt of a shoulder and sent him spinning. He then quickly moved away from that area as some Cork supporters were incensed by his actions.

The game was at a standstill at this stage, and then I saw something amazing. A friar who I later learned was Rev. Fr Nessan OFM of the Capuchin Order, for many years a Cork football selector, climbed up on the wall surrounding the pitch. Dressed in the distinctive brown robe of his order (including a white cord with three knots symbolising his vows of poverty, chastity and obedience), sandals and no socks, he began remonstrating with the crowd. He was soon joined by the Cork county board chairman Weeshie Murphy and Denis Conroy; eventually some semblance of order was restored and the game finished. However, the trouble continued as the players made their way from the ground. Some of the Kerry players were surrounded by a hostile crowd of what Dr Jim Brosnan later described as 'teenagers and teddy-boys'. Members of the Cork county board came to their rescue and brought some of the Kerry minor and senior players back to their hotel in their cars. This problem had arisen because the official Kerry cars which brought the players to the ground had to park over a mile away from where the players were to be collected after the game.

It was a strange day in Cork, and set in train a series of meetings between the two county boards and the Munster council. It was the beginning of a drive towards health and safety at GAA grounds, and in the following years more stewards, segregation of crowds and many other safety precautions were introduced.

3

THE CHALLENGE OF THE NORTHERNERS: COUNTY DOWN

A brilliant new team was about to change the whole landscape of the GAA. I first laid eyes on this Down team in Listowel early in 1960 when they played Kerry for the opening of the new sports field. Kerry hammered the Northerners, rattling in five goals in the process. The visitors were missing just one of their better players, Sean O'Neill. This win, I always believed, must have lulled Kerry into a false sense of security in relation to the worth of Down and would have huge ramifications for years to come.

No team from the six counties had ever won the All-Ireland. Unknown to all other counties, the foundations for the historic 1960 Down victory were put in place in 1958 when the county board gave permission to its secretary, Maurice Hayes (later a Senator), together with two former Down players, Barney Carr and Brian Devir, to form a three-man selection committee. These three men of great vision decided to plan for the long term and establish a five-year programme aimed at leading Down to an All-Ireland title. They proceeded to change the county championship format, making it much more competitive.

They spared no effort in treating the players on the county panel to the very best of everything, and the players responded with all-out effort and commitment never before associated with Down teams. Barney Carr became team manager, Danny Flynn team trainer, and former player Dr Martin Walsh team doctor. A management structure was now in place which in retrospect was the first of its kind for a county team; it was the blueprint for what we see in every county today.

While Kerry were slumbering, content with past glories and their 'catch and kick' style of play, Down were set to take the football world by storm, first winning the Wembley Tournament in London in thrilling fashion and later giving a magnificent display to defeat Cavan (2–16 to 0–7) to capture their first ever Ulster title on 9 August 1959 in Clones. However, this young, inexperienced Down team were no match for Galway in the All-Ireland semi-final; as their manager Barney Carr said afterwards, 'we learned more from this defeat than we ever knew and I firmly believe it will drive us on to greater things'. How right he was: Kerry would soon learn that this Down team was only just beginning to shine. They were now playing a brand of what I would term total, open, free-flowing football.

Kerry had their first warning of what they would face later in the championship when the Northerners beat them in the 1960 National League semi-final in Croke Park, 2–10 to 2–8. Down went on to capture their first ever league title, defeating Cavan in the final before a record crowd of 49,000. But the Sam Maguire was their goal. A second successive Ulster title was captured in 1960, as Cavan were once again defeated in the Ulster final. This time there was no slip-up in the All-Ireland semi-final: Offaly were overcome in a replay and the whole country was in a state of high expectation as Kerry and Down prepared to face each other in the All-Ireland final.

I was seated high up in the Hogan Stand in 1960 when Down stunned followers everywhere by beating hot favourites Kerry 2–10 to 0–8: the heaviest defeat ever suffered by Kerry in a final. It was an unforgettable experience because, as in later years when Tyrone introduced the swarming game, Down's style was something we had never seen previously. Before the game began they raced at full speed on to Croke Park, resplendent in this red and black strip. They had ten or twelve footballs and proceeded to run and race all over the place even before the game had begun. Kerry on the other hand ambled on to Croke Park; two footballs were used in the pre-match kick-around. The tension generated by the record attendance of over 80,000 spectators was unforgettable.

Kerry had failed miserably to learn from their National League defeat by Down, while the Down sideline men had their homework done well. They had left no stone unturned in their preparation of the team, and had even enlisted the coaching skills of former Meath football legend Peter McDermott, whose easygoing manner and vast knowledge helped to relax the players in the weeks preceding the big game.

Looking back now, it was abundantly clear as the game unfolded before me that I was witnessing the death of the traditional Kerry style of football: 'catch and kick'. This style had served Kerry well since their first All-Ireland title in 1903; they had added eighteen titles in the intervening years.

So what was the essence of the 'catch and kick' style that Kerry had fostered up to then? Well, to explain this I refer to an interview with the aforementioned Senator Maurice Hayes in Leinster House in 2007 as I researched material for a book on the life of Dr Eamonn O'Sullivan, the former Kerry trainer. The Senator's interview shows just how Kerry football thinking, preparation and style had stood still and how the northern county were streets ahead.

Referring to that 1960 final, Hayes said:

> One of the things we played on for that game was the fact that Dr Eamonn had a theory of zones on the field. All players kept to their places and did not move out of that zone, and so what we decided to do was introduce mobility into Gaelic football. So your full-back or half-back could move up-field with the ball and even make or get a score. I think it took Kerry a good while to come to grips with this change.

Hayes had hit the nail on the head in relation to the outmoded style Kerry had persisted with. He continued:

> In the late 1950s and early 60s there was a certain static quality about Kerry football. Now one of the things we attempted to do was play Kerry's great midfielder Mick O'Connell out of the game because our full-back Leo Murphy's kick-outs were so long and often passed the midfield area.

He also explained how they had singled out Kerry's centre-forward Tom Long for special attention, again demonstrating the amount of thinking the selectors had put into their preparations for the final. 'We reckoned Tom Long was the player who would win the match for Kerry if he wasn't held. Dan McCartan did a great job in marking him.' Then he hinted at another side of his team's tactics: 'And I must admit he probably held him in more ways than one.'

Mick O'Dwyer, who played in that 1960 defeat, was critical of the Down tactics. In one of the very many interviews I conducted with the Kerry great over the years, we discussed this aspect of their play. He paid generous tribute to Down for their tactical nous, athleticism, ball retention and off-the-ball running, but also claimed that they 'introduced a note of negativity which must have been pre-planned'.

Yellow or black cards weren't in use back then, so a team could indulge in consistent fouling without incurring any penalty other than the concession of frees. O'Dwyer alleged that Down exploited this to the maximum. He told me:

> They had no qualms whatsoever about fouling a player well out the field. I know they have always denied that deliberate fouling was part of their plan, but I played against them often enough to suspect that it most definitely was. After all, it was hardly a coincidence that they did it so systematically.

It was the first time also that I saw midfield players breaking the ball deliberately, as the Down pairing of Joe Lennon and Jarlath Carey attempted to thwart Kerry's Mick O'Connell and Jerdie O'Connor. It was the Down men who more often got the break, and this was not accidental in my opinion. It came about by intelligent positioning and their superior fitness, which accounted for the extra man being available when needed. Breaking the ball in the middle of the field and winning that break is now one of the most vital aspects of Gaelic football, and Down were the instigators of this new tactic unveiled against unsuspecting Kerry in that historic 1960 final.

Kerry were out-thought, out-fought and outrun by this fast-moving, fast-thinking, classy Down side and they simply had no answer, no Plan B. They were badly caught for fitness as the game unfolded, and while luck was not on their side – they conceded a very soft goal and later a penalty – Down were brilliant.

They were a superb side, and in James McCartan, Seán O'Neill, Paddy Doherty, Leo Murphy, Patsy O'Hagan and Captain Kevin Mussen I was looking at players who were some of the greatest I have ever seen. They changed the face of Gaelic football.

The sides met again in the 1961 semi-final; Down proved their previous year's win was no fluke and an ageing Kerry side once again suffered defeat, 1–12 to 0–9. Down were at the height of their glory, moving the ball with great speed, using the wings, kicking great scores and tremendously fit. They beat Offaly in the final that year; as their brilliant full-forward Seán O'Neill said to me in Caherciveen many years later, 'Beating Kerry on our way to both wins was the icing on the cake.'

Down were the instigators of modern football; they brought organisation, planning, preparation, special training techniques, dress, style and thinking into their game, and for Kerry the following years would prove traumatic as the Kingdom would be forced to adapt and move with the changing styles. It would take time, changes in management, heavy defeats and severe criticism from supporters, but in true Kerry style, as is their history, mistakes would be taken on board. A golden age for Kerry football was just around the corner.

I had my own experience of the 'catch and kick' style. In 1961, as was the norm, a Kerry trial match was held on the Monday preceding the final. It was 'the Probables' against 'the Possibles'. It was a massive crowd-puller, and I fail to understand why the same arrangement is not continued today. With all the pre-match publicity and hype I am convinced that it would attract a huge crowd and some worthy charity would benefit greatly from, say, a €5 entry fee. I was playing good club football at the time and was picked on the Possible team at wing-forward. Young and flying fit, I found it no problem to win plenty of ball and range across the field from wing to wing. However, I got a rude awakening at half-time when Dr Eamonn called me aside and warned me in no uncertain manner that if I did not remain in what he termed 'my sector of the field' I would soon be substituted. I was shattered, and when I was tied down to 'my sector' my opposite number easily got the better of me.

This was a wonderful example of just how far Kerry football had fallen behind the times. Dr Eamonn's philosophy had been highly successful up to this. His strict mantra was that when the ball entered a player's section, it was a simple man-to-man contest. Down had done their homework for those historic matches against the Kingdom, and they ran Kerry all over the wide open expanses of Croke Park.

Down have beaten Kerry each time the counties have met in Championship football. As late as 2010 Kerry's outstanding manager Jack O'Connor saw his superb side go under to the Northern men in the semi-final. However, I was present in Croke Park in 1963 when the Kingdom beat Down in the Home National League final, 0–9 to 1–5, before a record attendance of 57,180 spectators. Bernie O'Callaghan with four points and Tom Long with three were the stars in Kerry's first competitive win over the Mourne men. Niall Sheehy was captain that day, and his brother Sean Óg accepted the cup after a comprehensive victory in the 'final proper' against New York, 1–18 to 0–10.

1963 was the beginning of one of the bleakest periods in Kerry's football story, as a new force emerged from the West. Galway dominated the game for the next few years, winning three All-Irelands in a row (1964–6) and defeating Kerry on the way to each of those victories. John 'Tull' Dunne took over as trainer of the Galway side and, having studied the Down method of play, implemented a style that would completely demoralise Kerry.

The counties met in the 1963 All-Ireland semi-final; Kerry, as defending champions, were hot favourites. Galway won the game 1–7 to 0–8 with two late points from Seamus Leydon, and their style of play demonstrated how far Kerry were falling behind in their approach to the game. The Galway management team of Dunne, Frank Stockwell and Brendan Nestor knew that playing Kerry at their own game – high fielding, catch and kick – would not succeed, so they had their men drilled in the newer, modern style. The Galway team – stylish and slick, with a lovely mixture of youth and experience – moved the ball with great speed from defence to attack, keeping it low and chest-high as much as possible. It was the first time I saw the fisted pass used to such devastating effect: they were experts at it. Players were moving into open spaces all the time – no dilly-dallying on the ball – and displaying great fitness as Kerry players struggled to stay with them. The longer the game went on, the more openings began to appear in the Kerry defence.

Even worse was to follow when the sides met again in the 1964 All-Ireland final. Galway now had a very settled team. Nothing had happened in Kerry to improve the rapidly deteriorating situation, and the players approached the final in complete disarray. There were wholesale changes in the side and players were moved all over the place; star midfielder Mick O'Connell was chosen to line out at wing-forward. But it was not the players that lost the final; it was the style of play the Kingdom persisted with. Galway simply ran them off the field, winning 0–15 to 0–10.

That brilliant *Irish Times* reporter Paddy Downey summed it up the following day:

> The Kerry backs foundered about, bewildered by this high-powered Galway machine, the force of which they had experienced the previous

> year also. Indeed the wonder of it all was that the ball did not reach the net, not once but half a dozen times. For this, much credit must go to goalkeeper Johnny Culloty whose soundness between the posts was about the only bright spot in a dark day for Kerry football. The Kerry attack was the weakest fielded by the county in several years. Seldom has a Kerry team suffered such a thrashing at midfield, Mick Garrett and Mick Reynolds dominated the area from start to finish.

I was seated in the Hogan Stand that day. All the Kerry supporters were stunned at the vast gulf between the sides. Galway were brilliant.

Dr Eamonn O'Sullivan retired following the 1964 defeat (having stepped down for a time in 1960 – see below). He had given his county magnificent service over five decades. While he was not in charge every year, he was always available when the occasion demanded. He trained eight All-Ireland winning teams (1924, 1926, 1937, 1946, 1953, 1955, 1959 and 1962) and had a perfect record in finals. He remains the only person to have been involved in inter-county training for that incredible time span.

4

PLAYERS ON STRIKE!

While Down's win over Kerry in that 1960 final was well deserved, sensational events in Kerry off the field had not helped team preparations, and all was not well behind the scenes. Dr Eamonn O'Sullivan, Kerry's legendary trainer, was not in charge. He had opted out before the decider. While it is not perfectly clear why Eamonn stepped down, it is my information that he had requested better conditions for his players, such as improved medical back-up, higher travelling expenses and better meal selection.

His inability to attain these conditions, and the fact that he had not been taken to America with the team the previous year when they travelled as All-Ireland champions, meant that the good doctor was clearly and understandably unhappy with events and decided to resign. Eamonn never had a problem with not being a selector – this was the accepted situation for the trainer/coach back then – and did not look for any rewards for his time in charge, but he was a real players' man, always seeking better conditions for his men. Can you imagine this happening today? With all the media coverage Gaelic games receive, it would be headline news. In 1960 it was scarcely mentioned.

Unlike today, when players from Kerry, Dublin and the other successful counties earn big money for television ads, opening stores and newspaper interviews, and have trips to faraway places and all the trappings of success, in those days sponsorship was unheard of and the most any player could expect was a trip to London or New York. It's amazing to think now that Eamonn, as the team trainer, was excluded from these trips with his winning teams. Some of the players took grave exception to this and eventually decided to 'go on strike': yes, believe it or not, this was long before the Cork players went on strike in 2007. (The cause of that Cork strike was the issue of deciding who should pick the county senior team selectors.)

In 1960, two former Kerry All-Ireland medal holders – Johnny Walsh of Shannon Rangers and Gerald O'Sullivan of my own club, Killarney Legion – stepped in to prepare the team for the Down match. They applied the same training methods that had been in place for many years: 'catch and kick' was encouraged and players were directed to stay in their own zones.

Tom Long was one of Kerry's greatest players of that era, and years later in a lengthy interview he explained to me what had occurred.

> I had huge respect for the doctor and once I even went on strike for him. Eamonn was just the trainer and coach and not a selector, and once the All-Ireland would be over he would simply be forgotten about. There were very few perks going for players back then, unlike today. Eamonn was never even considered for a trip to the States or even England or anywhere in thanks. It wasn't right. A group of us players living and working in Dublin met and discussed this. We made a complaint to the Kerry county board and I think Eamonn agreed with our actions.

So Tom Long went on strike, and while his friends continued training in Dublin he as a teacher was on summer holidays at home in Kerry and refused to train with the team in Fitzgerald Stadium. I recall seeing him training on his own in the St Brendan's College field in New Road, Killarney. Eamonn was busy with his position as resident medical superintendent (RMS) in Killarney Mental Hospital and was not involved in any discussions. Johnny Walsh and Gerald O'Sullivan eventually met up with Tom and fixed up their differences. The strike was over, and the Dublin-based players came to join their team-mates in Killarney. Tom had no doubt that the absence of O'Sullivan and the interruption to training due to the strike contributed in a big way to the defeat by Down in 1960. 'We of course were badly beaten by Down and Eamonn was badly missed', Tom concluded. The attitude to the trainer after this definitely changed in Kerry, and while the term 'manager' is used today, the men responsible for preparing the county for Championship games are much more appreciated and have the final say in picking their own selectors – and rightly so.

It is not generally known that the strike by these Kerry players in 1960 in support of Dr Eamonn O'Sullivan was not in fact the first time such events had occurred within Kerry GAA circles. A much more serious strike took place way back in 1910, and probably cost Kerry another All-Ireland title to their name.

So just why did the Kerry players go on strike in 1910? In the previous year Kerry, captained by Tom Costello and with Dick Fitzgerald in their line-up, had beaten Louth in the final, 1–9 to 0–6. Louth were captained by the legendary Jack 'Sandman' Carvin, one of the Wee County's greatest ever footballers.

Kerry retained their Munster title in 1910, defeating Cork by 4 points to 2; Louth won out in Leinster and for the second successive year qualified to meet Kerry in the All-Ireland final. The game was fixed for 13 November at

Jones Road (now Croke Park). It was never played. Kerry refused to travel and Louth were awarded and accepted a walk-over from the Central Council.

The Great Southern Railway Company management of the time was regarded in Gaelic circles as hostile to the national game. In fact the *Dublin Leader* referred to them as 'the Great Sour Face Railway'. County boards around the country were severely handicapped when arranging matches or national demonstrations, then a feature of the Home Rule movement, by lack of co-operation on the part of the railway authorities. Excessive fares were set and proper travelling facilities were not provided. Kerry supporters travelling to big matches were often delayed for hours; however, it is reported that first-class facilities were laid on for rugby matches.

Consider the travelling facilities for our great players at the time and the terrible conditions they had to endure, and compare them with the luxury air and rail travel available to Kerry players today. It's like chalk and cheese. In the early 1900s two trains left Tralee for Dublin on a Saturday; however, the railway company would not permit the players to travel on the better, more comfortable 1.50 p.m. mail train. They always had to make the trip on the 3.20 p.m. train. This was as slow as a wet week and was generally overcrowded, arriving late in Dublin. Players in twos and threes were mixed with the other passengers. Confusion was increased in Killarney, where Saturday was market day and crowds of country shoppers boarded the train with baskets, bags, parcels and live chickens, turkeys or ducks. Can you imagine the conditions for men travelling to play in an All-Ireland final on the following day?

The late Tim Healy, former player and selector, told me in an interview some years before his death that his father, the legendary Paddy Healy of Headford, a farmer, would leave the fields or the bog on the Saturday and collect his boots and togs and a parcel of sandwiches wrapped in newspaper at home. The train would have an unscheduled stop near his home; he would clamber on board and maybe stand all the way to Dublin. On the return journey the following day the train would drop the great Kerry player off on the side of the track and it was back to his heavy farming work. There was widespread resentment at the attitude of the railway company, and the Kerry GAA county board sent a strongly worded letter asking for concessions including tickets at excursion rates for the ten officials travelling with the team. The following letter was received in reply by the secretary Michael Griffin (Listowel).

Kingsbridge, Dublin
November 9th, 1910

Dear Sir,
I am in receipt of your letter of yesterday's date and in reply beg to inform you that there will be sufficient room in the 3.20 pm train for the Kerry team travelling to Dublin on Saturday next, and it will not be necessary to provide a through coach as requested by you.

The team will be issued cheap tickets and the necessary order will be sent through Mr O'Toole, who is making arrangements. I regret that cheap tickets cannot be issued generally by the ordinary trains on Saturday and nothing better than the usual Saturday to Monday tickets can be given to those desirous of travelling to Dublin on the day.

The Company has arranged a special fast train at a reasonable fare on Sunday for the convenience of the Kerry people anxious to witness the match.

Yours truly
S. Cooper Chadwick

The opening paragraph incensed the Kerrymen. They decided not to travel, preferring to sacrifice the All-Ireland than to submit to the treatment meted out to them by the company. Kerry's action created a sensation and widespread disappointment. Many people thought that having beaten Louth the previous year, it was very foolish to throw away another All-Ireland title. Others, however, held that a great principle was involved, and that the time had arrived to take on the railway company. Public bodies in Kerry passed resolutions endorsing the attitudes of the players.

The Gaelic League in Ennis passed the following resolution: 'That we applaud the Kerrymen for the sacrifice they made in refusing to meet Louth, in order to bring to light the grave scandal which exists in the scant courtesy with which the chief railway Company of Ireland treats the various nationalist organisations in the matter of travelling facilities.'

The Munster counties fully supported Kerry's stand; many of them applauded it. However, at a meeting of the Dublin GAA county board the action of the Kerrymen was strongly condemned and a resolution was passed calling on the central council to expel Kerry from the association for five years. It should be recorded here that Cork stood four-square behind their great rivals, and a well-known Cork Gael was quoted as saying, 'If Kerry go into the wilderness, we go with them.' On 4 December Kerry's 'stand down', as it was being called, came before the Central Council and a resolution that the match be refixed was defeated by seven votes to six. Five Munster men including Kerry's Austin Stack, and Kilkenny's Jim Lawler were among the six minority votes. The title was awarded to Louth.

Kerry later issued a challenge to play Louth. There was no answer from Louth except to state that they were 'under no obligation to a bombastic challenge from Tralee'. The chairman of the Louth county board, however, wrote to the Dublin papers saying that Louth's second string would meet the Kingdom. Kerry answered that they were perfectly willing to meet Louth's second string provided Louth's seniors played Kerry on the same date and venue. Again no Louth reply. It was later stated at a central council meeting that as the final was not played, no funds were available and no medals would be presented to Louth. Then one paper scribe sarcastically suggested that Central Council should buy leather medals and present them to Louth.

A split in the association was barely avoided following a suggestion that a Munster body independent of the central council be established. Wiser heads prevailed and the unthinkable was not followed through. This historic Kerry–Louth affair was to have great benefits: there was a change in the attitude of the railway company and things did improve for the Kerry players.

It's only right and fitting that the present Kerry players travel in the utmost comfort to and from Dublin: God knows they are putting in enough time, sweat and effort, and deserve all the attention they get. However, we should never forget the magnificent stand taken at the huge expense of throwing away an All-Ireland by the men of 1910. Their actions should be applauded by all Kerry people. The heart and soul of Kerry football might be traced back to that year and the events of 'the stand down'.

5

SLOW CHANGE

Kerry's fortunes reached such a low ebb during the 1966/67 National League that in a game played in Tralee against Wicklow, at which I was present, the team were booed off the field at half-time. It was depressing stuff, and on that particular day it was hard to see light at the end of the tunnel.

When Jackie Lyne was appointed trainer of the Kerry team at the beginning of 1968 he was accepting a poisoned chalice. Lyne, a member of my own Killarney Legion club, was one of the most respected figures in the game, and it was a great move by the county board to appoint him. He came from a legendary football family – a farming family who resided in the townland of Cleeney, just outside Killarney. Jackie and his brothers Denny and Canon Mickey held All-Ireland medals and Denny had captained Kerry in the Polo Grounds, New York in 1947. Another brother, Ted, had helped Kerry to a junior All-Ireland win. Indeed, when Kerry won the 1953 Jubilee All-Ireland, Jackie was the only team member who had played in the county's previous win in 1946.

It was an inspired appointment by Dr Jim Brosnan and the board, and Lyne would go on to contest three finals, 1968, 1969 and 1970, winning two and also steering the county to two National Leagues. He had very little involvement in training prior to the Kerry job. In, 1967 he had trained our club to win the prestigious East Kerry O'Donoghue Cup, and as a member of that team I was fully aware of his capabilities. Quite simply, he had the touch, and his management skills and dealings with players on a one-to-one basis were first class. Little did I think as I trained under him that year with my club that two years later I would again be answering his whistle, but this time for the ultimate honour: that of preparing for an All-Ireland final with Kerry.

Lyne introduced more hand-passing, gave the players more freedom to leave their positions, had half-forwards defending (which was new to the Kerry style) and had Liam Higgins at full-forward where he would be used as a target man to get possession of the ball and hand-pass it to in-running forwards. Generally he brought much more modern thinking into the game.

However, despite Lyne's ability as a trainer and motivator of men, his success would never have come about only for the staging of a low-key, barely advertised trial game in Austin Stack Park, Tralee, in February 1968, organised at the request of Mick O'Dwyer. It was a game that would change the face of Kerry football. I was present on that bitter-cold day in Tralee, and looking back now I am of the opinion that without this game, Kerry football would have had one of its most barren spells ever.

The match was billed as Kerry Past versus Kerry Present and the result was the talk of the county. The Past beat the Present, 2–13 to 3–8. Mick O'Connell, Mick O'Dwyer and Seamus Murphy had retired, but so impressive was their form in this trial that Jackie Lyne persuaded them to return to the county panel. The greats returned and Kerry won two more All-Irelands and four National Leagues, all because this trial was held. O'Dwyer had retired two years previously and had been elected as one of the five Kerry selectors.

Those two teams were a 'who's who' of Kerry football. Kerry Past: Johnny Culloty, Pa Kerins, Joe Barrett, Sean Óg Sheehy, Mickey Walsh, Pat Moynihan,

Colm Callaghan, Mick O'Connell (1–0), Brian Sheehy, Bernie O'Callaghan, (0–1), Mick O'Dwyer (1–8), Derry O'Shea (0–1), Tom Long, Niall Sheehy, John 'Thorny' O'Shea (0–3). Kerry Present: Liam Higgins, Derry Crowley, Paud O'Donoghue, Seanie Burrows, Tom Prendergast, Declan Lovett, Pat Ahern, Mick Fleming, John Bunyan, John Saunders (0–2), Pat Griffin (0–1), Paudie Finnegan, Eamon O'Donoghue (1–0), Donie O'Sullivan (1–5), Tim Kelleher (1–0).

Liam Higgins, who played in goal in this trial, would go on to win two All-Irelands at full-forward, and the most amazing fact of all was that Mick O'Dwyer would be Kerry's top scorer for five of the next six seasons. Mick O'Connell topped the county's scoring list in 1969, scoring 0–15.

The Munster Championship was won, and Longford stood between Kerry and an All-Ireland final appearance. Mick O'Connell, Seamus Murphy and Mick O'Dwyer were playing great football, fully refreshed from their few years 'in retirement'; however, there were major problems in defence. Teddy Bowler, a recognised outfield player, had been pressed into service as goal-keeper. A total of five goals had been conceded to Tipperary and Cork in the Munster campaign, which forced the selectors to make a dramatic move.

Johnny Culloty, who had played his last game in goal in the Munster final defeat in 1966, was sensationally recalled to the team for the Longford game. Up until the eighties the base for all Kerry teams had been the now demolished Park Place Hotel in High Street, Killarney. There the teams stayed for collective training in the fifties, and all meals were served there. The hotel was owned by the O'Donoghue family: all great Kerry GAA people. Also the teams for all championship matches were picked in a little room at the rear of the hotel, and on the Monday prior to the Longford semi-final the selectors were in conclave. It was customary for crowds to gather outside the hotel on the street and await the announcement of the team from the genial secretary, Tadge Crowley.

There was always an air of excitement and a buzz among the diehard supporters when Tadge would appear at the hotel door. However, things were not as they seemed on this evening in 1968. Jackie Lyne and Tadge Crowley came out of the hotel, walked through the waiting crowd and made the five-minute journey to the home of Johnny Culloty. Their mission was to persuade the Legion man to come out of retirement and play the following Sunday. Culloty agreed to their request: he was still playing great football with his club and East Kerry, and as a dual player was playing in goal for the county hurlers. Another piece of the rebuilding jigsaw was completed.

Longford had won their first Leinster Championship, but Kerry's experience proved too much for them. Goals from Pat Griffin and Dom O'Donnell had Kerry ahead at half-time. Longford sensationally went ahead in the second half with goals from Tom Mulvihill and a penalty by Jackie Devine. As is their history, Kerry finished strongly and points from Mick O'Dwyer, Brendan Lynch and Din Joe Crowley won the day. The old adversaries Down once again awaited in the final.

I was sitting on the upper tier of the old Hogan Stand that September day in 1968 when Down once again proved the masters of the Kingdom in championship football. There was a massive media build-up to the final, and every Kerry supporter was longing for revenge following those defeats by Down in 1960–61. But it was not to be: in fact the game was all but over after just ten minutes as Down had jumped into an eight-point lead. It was a stunning start by the Mourne men. And the goal that set them on the way to victory is one of the most talked about of all time.

Years later in my role as Radio Kerry GAA analysist, I had the privilege of interviewing the man who scored it: Seán O'Neill, one of the greatest forwards to have played the game. Seán, a true unassuming gentleman, was in Kerry to take part in my programme *Terrace Talk*, and of course that famous goal came up for discussion. He explained what had happened forty years previously in Croke Rark at the Railway goal.

> We were 0–2 to 0–1 ahead. Peter Rooney cut in and shot over my head for a score. Now I have always made the point of following the ball when it went any way towards the opponent's goal. Ninety-nine times out of a hundred it will be a waste of energy; however, always expect the unexpected. And on that occasion the unexpected happened. The ball hit the post about five feet above the crossbar and it rebounded very fast back towards me.

I had very vivid memories of that amazing incident, and I put it to Sean that it appeared as if he was in fact falling as he went for the ball. He explained:

> Now I was in full stride and I realised in that split second that the ball was going to hit me below the knee, and if that happened I would not connect properly. Automatically I leaned my body forward and that is why it appeared as if I was falling forward. I connected perfectly as the ball came off the pitch and as if using the drop kick I stabbed at the ball and in an instant it was in the net. I never before or after scored a goal like this; I was lucky, it all happened in a split second.

It was all Down at this stage, and they came at Kerry in wave after wave of attacks. Two minutes after O'Neill's sensational goal Johnny Murphy cracked in another, and only for a series of brilliant saves by Johnny Culloty it would have been a cricket score.

Kerry did fight back to within four points before the end, but Down were not to be denied. Their captain Joe Lennon went off injured; Paddy Doherty, John Purdy and Colm McAlarney were outstanding. Mick O'Connell was moved controversially to full-forward as Pat Moynihan came in at midfield. Minutes before the end young Brendan Lynch faced up to a fourteen-yard free; his rocket of a shot to the Down net served only to put a better look on the scoreboard. It finished 2–12 to 1–13 and the Down dominance of the Kingdom continued.

There was an air of deep gloom around the county following this latest defeat, and many felt it had been another false dawn in the most depressing decade in Kerry football history. However, I recalled the words Jackie Lyne had said over a few pints in Jimmy O'Brien's famous pub in Killarney when he took over the team. 'I have made a promise to my family that I will win one All-Ireland before I pack the whole thing in, and I believe I have the men to do it.' He would be true to his promise: in the following two years he would lead Kerry to two glorious All-Ireland wins, and all my football dreams would come true as I became part of this Kerry squad and experienced the thrill of training with Kerry legends and savouring what I had marvelled at as a youngster – bringing the Sam Maguire Cup back to the county.

At the time of the 1968 final, Jackie Lyne was still learning about his panel of players. He was not ready for Down that year, and the Kerry style of playing was not yet a match for Down's. Kerry victories in the the following two years, 1969 and 1970 – beating Offaly and Meath in the finals – proved that Lyne had needed time to mould his side. If he had met Down again, it's fascinating to speculate how the result would have gone.

6

THE GOLDEN AGE: MICK O'DWYER

The early seventies was a disappointing time for Kerry followers: Munster Championship Final defeats by Cork in 1971, 1973 and 1974 and a heart-breaking All-Ireland defeat in a replay with Offaly in 1972. Johnny Culloty replaced Jackie Lyne as Kerry trainer in 1972; the term 'manager' had not yet entered the GAA vocabulary. Johnny retired as trainer following the '74 defeat by Cork, and the Kerry county board directed chairman Gerald McKenna to seek out a new trainer of the team. Gerald turned to Mick O'Dwyer from Waterville to fill the position. O'Dwyer was still playing club football with Waterville. McKenna's great persuasive powers worked, and on 22 March 1975 O'Dwyer was appointed trainer of the Kerry team. It would prove to be one of the most significant and momentous appointments in the history of Kerry football.

However, behind the appointment of Mick O'Dwyer was another fascinating Kerry story. Where else would it happen? Mickey Ned O'Sullivan was the chosen team captain for 1975 because his divisional team, Kenmare, had won the previous year's county championship. When this was confirmed early that year, he got a strange phone call from the then vice-chairman of the county board, the late Frank King. As Mickey explained to me, Frank told him 'You should know as captain that we have no trainer for the coming year. You have physical education qualifications and we want you to also be trainer of the team.'

Mickey Ned was reluctant to take on the job, but he had no other choice at that particular time. 'I knew it would not work, and being expected to lead the team on the field as captain and also off it as trainer was a non-starter', he told me. The county's degree of unpreparedness that year is shown by the fact that when Kerry played Dublin in a challenge match in Croke Park in early January, the team had no selectors as the county convention had not yet been held to vote in new men. It was the only time that a Kerry team played a game in Croke Park without the guidance of sideline mentors.

When the county convention was held in late January, Mick O'Dwyer's name was on the ballot paper for a position as selector and the delegates gave him an overwhelming vote of confidence, as he topped the poll with ninety-seven votes. Selected with him were Donie Sheehan (Killarney), Murt Kelly (Beaufort), Pat O'Shea (Cromane) and Denis McCarthy (Kenmare). So all was ready for the New Year: or was it? Mickey Ned was still determined not to combine the positions of trainer, player and captain. He persuaded the new selector, O'Dwyer, to accompany him to Gormanston to attend a coaching course given by Joe Lennon of Down. The Waterville man agreed after some persuasion, on condition that he would not have to sit an exam at the conclusion of the course. On the drive home, Mickey Ned began persuading O'Dwyer to take on the job of team trainer. The rest is history: Gerald McKenna followed up, met Mick in Tralee and the deal was sealed.

The new Kerry trainer was no ordinary man: I would rate him as one of the

Capturing the Heart and Soul

Some of Kerry and Ireland's best-known sports photographers choose a picture from their archives that captures the spirit of the county, the game, and its legendary players.

Páidí Ó Sé by Don MacMonagle

'I photographed Páidí Ó Sé as a player, a trainer, with his family, in business – and I was at his funeral. My photo of Páidí with his eight All-Ireland medals is probably my favourite. I asked him where he kept the medals, and his reply, verbatim, was, "In a *USAhhh* box under my mother's bed." There was I thinking they were locked away in a safe somewhere!'

Tadhg Kennelly
by Kerry Kennelly

'After Kerry defeated Cork in the 2009 All-Ireland final, Tadgh Kennelly – just returned from Australia – climbed up on the plinth and danced a jig, and the fans erupted. Then he hoisted the Sam skywards to huge applause, just as his late father, Tim Kennelly, did in 1979. Almost immediately, his expression changed from complete joy to near tears. I think this photo captures the bittersweet moment where Tadhg realised he had emulated one of the achievements of his father, a true great of Kerry football.'

Maurice Fitzgerald by Stephen McCarthy

'The picture was taken on a cold Wednesday night on the back pitch in Lewis Road, Killarney, where my local club, St Mary's of Caherciveen, were playing Gneeveguilla in a County League game. The previous weekend, I had covered their victory in the Munster Intermediate Championship. After the game, Maurice Fitzgerald, who was managing St Mary's, joked that he would tog out the following Wednesday, as they were planning on resting a number of players. I asked one of the players to give me a heads-up if he heard anything, and late the night before, the message came through – Maurice would be togging out. After racing from Dublin to Killarney, I saw one of the greatest players of all time – the man I had been in awe of growing up – grace the field in the blue and white sash of my beloved St Mary's.'

Jack O'Connor by Michelle Cooper Galvin *(opposite)*

'After Kerry won the All-Ireland in 2004, I travelled all the South Kerry area, including every school, with manager Jack O'Connor and some members of the team. We went onto the beach at St Finian's Bay, his home area, and while taking some shots on the rocks, a storm blew in from the Atlantic and we had to run for cover. As Jack was ahead of myself, I just took the photo.'

Leo Griffin by Brendan Landy

'Legendary Kerry bagman and water-boy Leo Griffin is ordered to the line by referee Thomas Maher in a Munster Championship game against Limerick in 1989. The Tralee man, who died in 2015 aged seventy-five, will forever be associated with the era when Kerry racked up eight All-Ireland titles under Mick O'Dwyer between 1975 and 1986. O'Dwyer described him as "a great and loyal friend to me and Kerry football".'

© BRENDAN LANDY, LANDY PHOTOGRAPHY LISTOWEL

© JOHN STACK

Keith Hughes and Sean Carr by John Stack

'Keith Hughes and Sean Carr, after the battle of playing and winning a North Kerry Championship medal for the first time. The release of emotion and joy is evident in this picture. Winning with your club is special – very special.'

Colm Cooper by Domnick Walsh *(opposite)*

'Kerry's Colm Cooper in action against James McCarthy of Dublin in the 2015 All-Ireland final in Croke Park. The rain was lashing into my sports lens, which stopped working – I had to move fast to get it started again. I used a back-up lens to capture this image from close to the goal mouth. For the rest of the match I worked on in the rain, so wet inside and outside that when I stood up, pools of water flowed down my legs and into my boots. Still, I love my job as a photojournalist, and to work with people like Colm Cooper, who show a lot of respect to me and my colleagues, makes it all worthwhile.'

Sam and friends by John Reidy

'As a newspaper photographer in Kerry, I had often witnessed the excitement of a player-accompanied visit of the Sam Maguire Cup to a GAA summer camp. Here, I set my camera's functions to create the buzz and fuzz of excitement, and the children of the Castleisland Desmonds GAA Club supplied that lovely splash and swirl of colour. After the photograph had appeared in the paper, I was having a pint in a local pub and the owner came over to me and said, "I don't like saying this to you, but I couldn't make out any of the children's faces in that photo … Are you all right?" I wasn't able to answer him for a while.'

Kieran Donaghy by Bryan O'Brien

Kerry goalscorer Kieran Donaghy is mobbed by fans after the 2006 All-Ireland Senior Football Final between Mayo and Kerry in Croke Park.

Sean Walsh by Kevin Coleman

This magnificent Kevin Coleman photograph of Kerry's Sean Walsh and Dublin's Brian Mullins reaching high into the clouds in the 1979 All-Ireland final is recognised as one of the most iconic ever taken. It symbolises a beautiful skill in Gaelic football: high fielding. Páidí Ó Sé (RIP), at number five, looks on.

Bryan Sheehan by Eamonn Keogh

'Bryan Sheehan is the master of dead ball situations, and given a chance to convert a free from anywhere in the field, he is almost certain to bury it. On his live radio commentary, Weeshie described this moment from the 2009 Kerry County Championship final between South Kerry and Dr Crokes as the longest free he had ever seen kicked in Fitzgerald Stadium without the aid of a wind.'

Sam on the summit by Valerie O'Sullivan

Mícheál Ó Muircheartaigh holding the oldest All-Ireland medal, dating back to 1887, and lifting the Sam Maguire Cup on the summit of Carrantuohill. With Mícheál is legendary Kerry footballer and Glenflesk man Seamus Moynihan and mountain guide Piaras Kelly of Kerry Climbing (right). The 'Sam to Summit' event, in aid of the Alan Kerins Projects, saw representatives, players and medals from thirty-two counties reach the top of Ireland's highest mountain.

Mick O'Dwyer by Christy Riordan

'This picture of Mick O'Dwyer was taken the evening before the unveiling of his statue [by sculptor Alan Hall] in Waterville. Myself and Micko have been great friends down through the years, so we took a good few photos with himself, the Waterville players and the committee.'

Bringing Sam home by Mike Brosnan

Kerry captains Kieran O'Leary and Fionn Fitzgerald with the Sam Maguire at Ross Castle, Killarney, on the Tuesday morning after winning the All-Ireland in 2014.

five greatest players I have seen playing with Kerry, and I have seen them all since 1955. I had played against Mick in county finals and played and trained with him during my time on the Kerry panel in the late sixties. He had won every honour the game had to offer, including four All-Ireland medals: two as a defender and two as a forward, a very rare occurrence. He won eight National League medals and twelve Munster championship medals; he was voted Footballer of the Year in 1969 and was top scorer in Ireland in 1969 and 1970. Now, in his new position, he was to change the face of modern football. His training methods would be revolutionary, combining swift hand-passing with gruelling non-stop running. His mantra was simple: we will be fitter than any other team in the country. As trainer/manager he would guide Kerry to ten All-Ireland finals, winning eight. It seems as if forty-one years have passed in the blink of an eye since we witnessed the birth of what many shrewd judges recognise as the greatest football team the game has ever seen. Mick O'Dwyer, Mickey Ned O'Sullivan, 1975, Croke Park, the Dubs, the Sam Maguire Cup – these will forever be remembered when Kerry football history is discussed.

However, it was with his club, Waterville, that Mick cut his teeth as a trainer and manager of men: a fact he alluded to in one of the many interviews I conducted with him over the years.

> When Gerald McKenna first approached me with that offer to train Kerry I was very surprised, really. I was also unsure of myself, as the only experience I had was with the own club Waterville, whom I had trained in the sixties. While the challenge was very exciting and even irresistible I could see all the problems I might face straight away and I was very reluctant to take on the task. In Kerry you are expected to get

> results every single year, defeat is not an option and supporters are very intolerant of failure. The supporters can often be savage in their criticism, so to cover myself I agreed to take on the job for just one year.

That 'one year' would of course stretch into twelve.

The methods Mick put into practice to train Waterville were very similar to those that would later win all those All-Irelands for Kerry. Sean O'Shea was a member of the great club side that played in three Kerry county senior finals, 1968–70, and was lavish in his praise of O'Dwyer when he spoke to me last year.

> We had a very small pool of players and we all lived very close to each other, and when Mick took over the training our whole lives literally changed. He was a wonderful leader of men: once we even went fifty competitive games in a row losing just once. I lived in Derrynane, about seven miles from Waterville; I was a fisherman and every day of the week I would haul ninety lobster pots by hand: it was hard, gruelling work but I never missed a night's training simply because Mick O'Dwyer led by example and we all followed.

Sean described some of O'Dwyer's training methods, all based on getting every member of the panel to the same level of fitness.

> Our pitch was under construction for a few years, and he would bring us to the local golf course where we played football: this would be after a long session of running on the beach, up and down the sand dunes, sprinting, every man anxious to beat the others and impress

> O'Dwyer. It was savage stuff. Piggyback was a big thing with him to strengthen the legs; press-ups and more sprinting. He was huge on discipline, never one to be late himself: you would get extra runs if you were not on time and any fellow that was out for a few drinks the night before really suffered … he banned smoking, and believe it or not even to this day when I meet Mick I will never smoke in his company. I respected the man so much and still do.

While Waterville lost those three county finals, it remains one of the greatest ever achievements for such a small village down in South Kerry to have contested those deciders. In fact I firmly believe that if they had met club sides in the finals they would have won at least one or two. However, it was the divisional side East Kerry that opposed them. I was a member of that East Kerry side: we had the pick of fourteen clubs from the district and really we were the closest you would get to an inter-county side. I have vivid memories of those games and especially of O'Dwyer playing at centre-forward for Waterville; he was a giant among men. Strong as an ox, brave as a lion, a wonderful all-round footballer, his determination, leadership and will to win were simply frightening. He was now ready to transfer all those magnificent qualities to the Kerry senior team. I firmly believe his leadership qualities were far more important than his training methods.

When O'Dwyer began his training career with the Kerry seniors in March 1975, he inherited much of the work that outgoing trainer Johnny Culloty had instigated during his term. The Killarney Legion man had been responsible for introducing such players as Paudie O'Mahony, Mikey Sheehy, Páidí Ó Sé, Ger O'Keeffe, Ger Power, Jimmy Deenihan and John Egan to the senior set-up. In these men can be found another secret of Micko's success: youth.

The All-Ireland winning teams of 1969–70 were broken up, and one of the players discarded was Seamus Mac Gearailt. Seamus later recalled:

> When he took over in 1975 he made the decision to go for youth and a good few of the older lads were left off the panel. Of course we were not too happy about this and we believed we had much more to offer. However, looking back, O'Dwyer was correct: he went with a youth policy, beat Dublin in 1975 and that group went on to become the great side they were.

Only three players from the 1969–70 victories remained on Micko's new panel – Donie O'Sullivan, Brendan Lynch and John O'Keeffe – and their experience would prove invaluable. O'Dwyer had been the trainer of the Kerry under-21 side that lost to Cork in the Munster Championship in Caherciveen the previous year (1974). He had seen the great potential in these young players, and recalled later:

> They had wonderful skills. Mikey Sheehy was amazing, he could do anything with a football, but he was totally unfit, overweight and struggled as the game went on. All of those under-21 players who would make up the basis of the senior side the following years had great possibilities provided they were ready to knuckle down and put in some really hard training: this was foremost in my mind for them.

It has been fascinating for me over the years, having met and interviewed most of this great team, to hear them recall and discuss just what Mick O'Dwyer brought to the new set-up. In fact I was in a privileged position, as

I lived just five minutes' walk from Fitzgerald Stadium in Killarney and many the winter or summer evening I spent with friends sitting in the stand, seeing Micko put his men through their paces. It was open training back then, of course: unlike today.

When training began in March 1975 for Micko's young lions, the new regime hit the players like a ton of bricks. Mikey Sheehy recalled:

> There was nothing in his mind but winning an All-Ireland from the very first training session: it was brutal stuff and at one stage we trained twenty-seven nights in a row. I had never before been put through such training; it was as near professional as you could get. Mick knew well that he had the makings of a very good side and his first priority was to get the fitness levels up, and he certainly achieved that. It was without a shadow of doubt all this training that won the All-Ireland for us in 1975.

Sheehy went on to play under O'Dwyer until 1987, winning eight All-Ireland medals, eleven Munster medals and three National Leagues, and scoring the massive total of 29 goals and 205 points.

Mickey Ned O'Sullivan, who had played a major part in convincing O'Dwyer to take over as trainer, recalled for me the first night in Fitzgerald Stadium:

> I made out a rough session for him. He took it. It was the only time he ever consulted. He did the session with us. He came to me and said 'What did you think of it?' I said it wasn't half hard enough really. I had become obsessed at that stage. It was the only chance there'd be

> of captaining a team to an All-Ireland.
>
> The next night he crucified us. He never asked me again. We had the same basic training for the next ten or twelve years. He had enough cop-on to take control and did it his own way. Take it or lump it.

He ran them into the ground and he altered Mickey Ned's passing style, having seen Kerry run into a lot of walls in that year's league semi-final against Meath.

> Dwyer came in then and made us kick it. That made the difference. He made you kick the ball long. Same spaces but quick release. Nothing changed after that.
>
> He had an innate cuteness which came to a certain level. It wouldn't be rational – it was passionate and a gut feeling. He knew Spillane needed a bit of media and he could handle him. And Paudie Lynch, say, was quiet, a players' player, and a craftsman. No fuss. Same with John Egan. Ogie would be buzzing. Brendan Lynch would be quiet but he had fierce fire. No geeing-up needed. Powery had the same. John Egan needed a bit of a stir. This was how Mick would look at it. Basic but his finger was on the pulse.
>
> He would leave me take charge in the dressing room and do the pep talk. When I left the captaincy he never left anyone else do it after that, apart from Páidí in 1978. He grew in confidence with success.

And there would be plenty of that.

Pat Spillane, another man who won eight All-Irelands during the O'Dwyer era, had another take on what was developing.

> His regime was totally different from anything I had experienced before; of course the sessions were hard but we were young and fit and we were well able to take them. In the run-up to the All-Ireland final against Dublin we were training five times a week. Of course as the years and the miles mounted up I have far more painful memories of what O'Dwyer put us through. Mick was a very strict disciplinarian: whatever time training was due to start you had to be there well beforehand. And he was his own man; he called all the shots. There were several physical training instructors on the team, including John O'Keeffe, Jimmy Deenihan, Ogie Moran and myself, but he never once consulted us for any sort of advice or direction. Mick did it his own way from start to finish.

I once asked Mick whether having physical instructors on the team was a big help to him.

> No, I never consulted with any of them; if I did my position would definitely have been undermined. I had my own theories as regards training men; these fellows were young, keen and eager for work and they took everything I threw at them.

The biggest influence was an unlikely one. A friend by the name of Billy Behan was a Manchester United scout in Ireland in the 1950s, and organised a trip for O'Dwyer to meet Matt Busby in the off season. Mick brought back the idea of distance running and modern exercises, but couldn't implement a weights programme because no facilities were available.

But sure I looked everywhere to learn. I even went to a training course under Kevin Heffernan [the Dublin trainer], would you believe, but didn't take a whole lot from that. There were actually exams to be sat the following morning. The night before I said to Mickey [Ned O'Sullivan], 'To hell, we'll get out of here.' But Busby was the reason, more than anything, why I did take over Kerry.

***

Everything was now in place; the stars, it appeared, were aligned for another assault on the All-Ireland. Dublin were the reigning All-Ireland champions; Cork had been one of the highest scoring All-Ireland winners in 1973.

And so the youngest Kerry team ever fielded in a championship began their voyage to Croke Park against Tipperary in Clonmel on 15 June 1975: always a very difficult venue to visit. The home side had scored 7–18 in the first round against Limerick, so the warning signs were there. The scores were level at half-time; Tipperary went ahead shortly after the restart and then the Kerry selectors made a master move. John Egan was brought to the forty; he scored 2–2 between the fourteenth and seventeenth minutes and sealed the result. Egan, such a beautifully balanced, skilful and brave player, told me in an interview, 'I loved the freedom of the forty and O'Dwyer had us in tremendous shape. Remember, seven players were making their championship debuts that day so we were relatively very inexperienced.'

Cork awaited Kerry in the Munster final and they were hot favourites to achieve three titles in a row. Living just a stone's throw from Fitzgerald Stadium in Killarney, I was fortunate to be in a position to attend the training sessions every evening (no lock-out back then), and what was unfolding was mind-boggling. Never before had a Kerry team trained for twenty-seven consecutive nights. It was brutal stuff as O'Dwyer punished his men and pushed them beyond the limits with rounds of the field, sprinting wire to wire, and flat-out thirteen-a-side games. Very few sports journalists gave Kerry a chance of winning, but within the squad spirits were high.

Kerry dominated the game against Cork, winning 1–14 to 0–7. Pat Spillane got a fortunate early goal when a Cork defender deflected the ball into his own net. It was scintilling stuff played in hot, humid conditions before a crowd of 43,295. Jimmy Deenihan held Jimmy Barry-Murphy scoreless, and when he did foul the Cork star in the square Paudie O'Mahony saved the resultant penalty.

Páidí Ó Sé was fortunate that he was not sent off when he decked his man with a right upper-cut for what he described afterwards as 'a bit of verbal intimidation'. Cork were completely demoralised as the Kingdom strolled to their fifty-fourth Munster Championship.

Micko had the scent of victory in his nostrils, and he continued to drive the boys in training with ferocious determination. Sligo were Kerry's next opponents, visiting the capital for their first championship game in Croke Park since 1928. The legendary veteran Mickey Kearins was their side but the young Kerrymen brushed them aside with little difficulty, 3–13 to 0–5. John Egan with 2–2 and Pat Spillane, 1–1, led the rout. The Spa man Paudie O'Mahony saved another penalty, diving to his right at the Railway End to keep another clean sheet. No goal conceded so far by Kerry in the championship.

Dublin had scored 3–13 against Derry in the other semi-final and the whole country awaited the final with great expectation. The Kerry captain Mickey Ned O'Sullivan tells a great story in relation to the lead-up. A teacher, he got permission from O'Dwyer to embark on a holiday he had booked the previous year. 'After the Sligo game in the lead-up to the final we trained for thirty-five nights, but I missed a lot of that,' he told me. 'I was touring around Europe with a friend and I trained in Paris, Austria, Switzerland, Italy, the Rhine Valley, and on top of the Alps. Any place I could find a field I would tog out. Micko knew well that I would come home in top condition, and I did.'

Sunday, 28 September 1975: it rained heavily in Dublin that day. I travelled up to the game with my late brother Genie and friends; the atmosphere was electric as the sides raced on to the field. O'Dwyer had the lads in magnificent shape. They were sharp, fit and hungry; I have never seen fifteen Kerry footballers jumping out of their skins as that young side all those years ago.

Just three minutes after the throw-in Gay O'Driscoll, the Dublin defender, failed to collect the ball. John Egan was on it like a panther and, as if in slow motion, I can still see him skip round the backs with that beautiful ballet-like motion. His bullet of a shot, beautifully placed out of Paddy Cullen's reach, sent the raindrops dancing off the net at the Canal goal. Valentia's Ger O'Driscoll came on for Mickey Ned, who had been brutally knocked unconscious by a Dublin elbow, and Ger also raised the green flag.

Once again the youth, speed, skill and Kerry tradition were there for all to marvel at, and the final score was Kerry 2–12, Dublin 0–11. Paudie O'Mahony had not conceded a goal in the championship, and John Egan finished top scorer for the year with 5–7, followed by Pat Spillane with 2–8. Ger Power was voted Man of the Match.

The county was in seventh heaven. Thousands turned out to greet the team when they returned to Killarney on the Monday, and something about this bunch of Kerry bachelors had touched the hearts of their loyal followers. The streets were jam-packed, and as the lorry carrying the team inched its way at a snail's pace down Plunkett Street, confetti was scattered on them from the windows high above. The now demolished Park Place Hotel in High

Street was the destination as always for the speech making, and a hoarse Mick O'Dwyer made the startling announcement that 'This bunch of players could go on and win ten All-Irelands.' In fact the majority of this team won seven more All-Irelands and thirteen Munster Championships.

It was the beginning of a golden era in Kerry's long and glorious football story. Forty-one years have passed, but for me it seems like only yesterday. Sadly, Páidí Ó Sé, Tim Kennelly and John Egan have been called to their eternal reward, but for those of us who saw them and their teammates grow and develop into magnificent players, they will live forever. Those men were special: they were magnificent ambassadors for the Kingdom, and captured the hearts and souls of Kerry supporters all over the world.

***

O'Dwyer's training is now the stuff of legend in Kerry, everywhere football is discussed in the county – and boy, it's discussed morning, noon and night, summer and winter. Talk to any of his players from that era and they will have stories to tell about their time under the Waterville maestro.

The name Eoin 'Bomber' Liston is revered in GAA circles: this Ballybunion-born, six-foot-three-inch giant was the final part of the O'Dwyer jigsaw when he was introduced to the Kerry senior team in 1978. In a magnificent career, 'Bomber' won seven All-Ireland medals, nine Munster medals and four All-Star awards.

Micko's savage training remains forever etched in his memory:

> Mick was a stickler for time and he was always first out on the field himself. A few kick arounds with the footballs first and then two laps

> of the field, sprinting the last seventy yards. This was the warm-up: walk around for a few minutes and then another lap of the field, jog and sprint on the whistle; this was repeated a few times, walk around, and then came the wire-to-wire – lung-busting stuff. Three players lined up backs to the sideline wire and a full-out sprint across the width of the field, touch the wire on the far side, quick turn and flat out back to the start. He would often put in the fastest sprinters with the fatties [Eoin's own word!] and show just how far you were trailing fellows. Then he would put the fatties against the fatties and more wire-to-wire, over and back a few more times, flat out, gasping for breath, legs buckling but no surrender.

Recovery time between these wire-to-wires was short: a walk around the field behind the goals, then they would jog together around the field again and Mick would get a group of three to sprint the last thirty yards to the end line. Then more sprints: line up in groups on the end line and sprint on the whistle out and back thirty yards; this was repeated ten times. It was ferocious stuff, but there was method in the madness of O'Dwyer, as he once told me.

He would send his teams on long-distance runs. He knew he was not developing marathon runners. He did it for one reason: character.

> That's the way you'll test the mentality of a player: distance stuff, hard work … if he's a player that will give you 100 per cent, he'll go the distance. That's why we got to where we were with Kerry, with the amount of work we did in Fitzgerald Stadium. We did a pile of work all year round there. Those players gave me everything and they had wonderful character, but we also played a huge amount of football.

Bomber remembered:

> In the middle of all that stamina-building running we would break for a football session. Some nights we would have backs and forwards, six men on six, with O'Dwyer kicking in the ball high and low between the pairings, and often I at full forward would be marking John O'Keeffe at full back, and you simply had to beat your man for the ball and if not you were shown up, and someone else would take your place. Micko loved matching off players against each other both at running and football. He was brilliant at getting the very best out of every single individual; this was one of his strongest points. Some nights we would have thirteen-a-side matches, full blooded, each player trying to show up the other.

So was it true, as many people said, that tactics were not Micko's strong point and were never discussed? According to Liston:

> Of course we worked on tactics, but they were very simple and straightforward and remember, Weeshie, the game was completely different back then: no swarming, never fourteen men behind the ball as we see today, and basically every man for himself. However, we used our heads and skills in a big way. Mick was great into keeping space; he was always on to us about running into the open spaces: something, I later learned, he picked up from Dr Eamonn O'Sullivan, the former trainer. He would say, 'Ye're like Mrs Brown's cows, all bunching together in the middle of the field: keep out to the wings, let the centre open, no bunching.'

> And it worked: he always insisted we kick the ball long and fast, always giving the man receiving it a 60/40 chance of winning it. During all my years at full-forward one of the corner-forwards would rove out and the ball would be kicked into that space and it was up to me to win it: that was the tactic. Simple but effective. And of course it was the era of hand-passing and we exploited this to the fullest, moving the ball very quickly by both hand and foot.

The one thing that fascinated me when attending the training sessions was the awesome speed of all the players from one to fifteen, as the year unfolded. For the very first time, to the best of my knowledge, the Kerry defenders – in particular the full-back line – were faster that even the half-forward line. He literally built his team from the back. The full-back line that won the 1975 All-Ireland was in my opinion the fastest the game has ever seen, and that includes right up until today.

Ger O'Keeffe (right corner-back), John O'Keeffe (full-back) and Jimmy Deenihan (left corner-back) were all wonderful athletes. Ger, the fastest of them all, was a former All-Ireland college sprint champion. O'Dwyer would match him with some of the slower players, wire-to-wire: Ger, lean and mean, leading over and back, over and back again, barely sweating; the rest out on their feet. O'Dwyer, a big grin on his face, loved this: testing their character, the few watchers in the stand silent, mesmerised by the speed, commitment and effort. In later years Mick Spillane and Paudie Lynch, also speedsters, would deputise in the full-back line.

The Bomber again:

> He always told us that you must win every ball, show total disregard

> for your own personal safety. Every man was responsible for marking his own man: be tight, always know where your man is, attack the ball at all times. He kept repeating all of this continuously until it came to us automatically, we were playing with instinct, and this was the way he had played his entire career himself.

I had played with and against Micko and had watched as he played in all his All-Ireland finals and the man was a magnificent footballer, but it was his sheer bravery, enthusiasm and will to win that remains etched in the memory. As I watched him train his young lions I could see that everything he taught them was from the O'Dwyer manual. It was completely different from all previous Kerry trainers who had gone before him. However, his most lasting legacy was his ability to keep his players motivated, fit and possessing the will to win at all costs.

From 1975 until his retirement in 1989, as his players achieved undreamt-of success, celebrations and holidays to far away places were the norm, and with this came partying, functions, drinking and socialising. But he always got them right for the championship.

The players dreaded going back into training unfit following the winter break – they knew that O'Dwyer would run them into the ground – so they began training before official training commenced. Groups of them would travel to Banna beach and pound the miles in an attempt to shed the winter pounds. Ger Lynch was working in Cork and his winter route was pounding the miles around Cork city; Paudie Lynch always had his own training done before he arrived in to Micko, and would be regularly be seen on cold winter evenings doing circuit training around Dunloe castle, near his home in Beaufort.

Liston told me:

> You would suffer really bad if he thought you were after a session of drink. After Munster finals and All-Ireland semi-finals he would bring in the beer men for special training, fellows like Páidí, Tim Kennelly, John Egan, Mikey Sheehy, Paudie Lynch, myself and a few more … many the night I saw fellows vomiting behind the goals as we paid for our good times, but he had this rare gift of having every single player at his peak for the big games.

Mick believed that his players should benefit in some monetary way from their achievements: he was always one step ahead of the Croke Park authorities in this aspect of the game. After all, he was also a very successful businessman, owning a hotel, bar and nightclub in Waterville. He had his players wearing specific sportswear, and set up photographs of the panel that were then sold around the county. A commissioned portrait of one of his winning teams helped finance a foreign holiday. He organised his players to stand around a Bendix washing machine wearing just towels wrapped around their waists, and this photograph was used in a full page of a national newspaper.

The GAA authorities were privately fuming at this blatant attempt to flout the laws of the association, but Micko was opening up a new world of commercialism, and exploited every loophole. He was ahead of his time in this respect and his players benefited hugely, travelling to exotic holiday destinations all over the world.

Now the GAA are knocking on every door in their quest to bring in more money: nothing is sacred and foreign holidays are taken for granted, as is every form of commercialism on the part of players and authorities. The big word in GAA circles is sponsorship, and Mick O'Dwyer was the trend-setter in this respect as well as the greatest manager the game of Gaelic football has ever known.

Ger O'Keeffe was a member of O'Dwyer's team from 1974 to 1982, winning three All-Ireland medals and five Munster medals. He was also a selector with Jack O'Connor's All-Ireland winning sides, and says that O'Dwyer was easily the best man manager he trained under.

> I loved going to training when he was in charge: he brought a whole era of professionalism to Kerry football. He was always shown great respect from the players and we were all aware that he had been a great player himself. He treated everyone the same; however, I sometimes suspected he had a few favourites and the only time you had a bit of tension between him and the players was when a fellow was dropped or taken off during a game, but otherwise he was brilliant.

Ger has memories of the savage training sessions: 'I can remember going down to the Park Place Hotel in Killarney for our meal after training and fellows were unable to eat their T-bone steaks, they were so sick and shattered after the session, and Mick would get a great kick from this.'

O'Dwyer worked with some great selectors during his time in charge: men like Joe Keohane, Liam Higgins, Tim Kennelly, Donie Sheehan, Dave Geaney, Pat O'Shea, Kevin Griffin and others, who knew their football upside down. So how did he get on with these men? According to Ger O'Keeffe:

> I never saw him arguing in public with a selector: maybe they had disagreements behind closed doors when they were picking teams,

> but he had a great way with all people. Now of course he liked to have a big say in the final selection of the teams: after all, he was the man who knew the players' form better than anyone else. I never saw him get into any conflict with opposition selectors or trainers on the sideline; he always fought his corner but he never insulted a person or made little of anyone. I will go as far as to say that Mick O'Dwyer was and still is one of the finest gentlemen you would ever meet. Due to him the players of that era are massively respected all over Kerry and beyond, and everywhere I go people love asking about the Mick O'Dwyer era.

I can recall Eamon Dunphy and John O'Shea of GOAL – both of whom were writing sports columns for Dublin newspapers at the time – togging out and training with the team on a few occasions. It's impossible to imagine that happening today. Mick never fell out with reporters; he was always available to them and I heard him say once when we were discussing interviews, 'Don't forget, lads: the pen is mightier than the sword.'

He was always great at bouncing back after defeat. He was brilliant at lifting the morale of players, and always had goals to reach. The defeat by Offaly – the Seamus Darby goal in 1982 – hit him hardest of all, but he went away, recovered, got the players together again and went on to win the All-Irelands of 1984, 1985 and 1986. This was an amazing achievement, and only O'Dwyer could have done it.

It wasn't just Kerry people who admired Mick. Eugene McGee, who trained Offaly to deprive Kerry of that historic five-in-a-row win in 1982, wrote beautifully of the Waterville man in his 2014 autobiography.

For me the most important aspect of his career was his own personality. He was a lovely man, a term rarely attached to a GAA manager I admit, but the test is that hardly anyone disliked the Waterville maestro; he never seriously annoyed people in the GAA including the other managers the he encountered.

You simply loved having a chat with Mick O'Dwyer because he loved Gaelic football as a passion and that always overcame any disappointment and sorrows he endured through football in his long career. When he finished with Kerry he trained Kildare, Laois and Wicklow and everywhere he went in all those counties Mick O'Dwyer was respected and liked to an extraordinary extent bearing in mind his age and long time at the game. It proved the man's amazing personality that allowed him become immune to the sort of rows we often get in the GAA.

So many managers at the present time could learn a lot from Mick O'Dwyer's behaviour and the demeanour and the manner in which he conducted himself whether winning or losing. He never imposed a media ban either. Like everyone in the GAA I was very fond of Mick O'Dwyer and I was always glad to meet him at a match or a function. A lifelong teetotaller, he was a most sociable person and would talk forever.

Finally the Offaly man sums up Mick as perfectly as anyone has ever done, and echoes my own thoughts:

He was a wonderful adornment for the GAA and is definitely entitled to be acclaimed as the best manager in GAA history because of the diverse range of his contribution across several counties. If class is a measurement of success then Mick was the very best.

Mick O'Dwyer played in ten senior All Ireland finals (including one replay); he was trainer/manager of Kerry in ten senior All-Ireland finals, winning eight, but people are inclined to forget that he also trained Kerry under-21 sides in four consecutive All-Ireland finals, 1975–78, winning three and losing the other by a point. He was the manager of six Munster Railway Cup winning teams. It's amazing that he had a direct input as a player or manager/trainer in twenty-four senior and under-21 All-Ireland football finals.

According to Ger O'Keeffe, whom I spoke to as I researched this book:

> It is almost impossible to insult him or rise his temper. He is always in great humour: his placid manner, his wonderful zest for life and his sheer enthusiasm for all aspects of his life is something I have rarely seen in others. Even right up until today I love meeting him: an hour in his company and you will come away feeling much better for the time spent. Yes, I will say he is one of my favourite people.

His great friend the late Owen McCrohan, the man who wrote a superb biography of Mick, finished the book with the following tribute.

> If there is any truth in the old adage which suggests that 'a soft answer turneth away wrath', then Mick O'Dwyer is the living embodiment of that principle. His boyhood friend Eric Murphy says of him 'You could have an argument with him and you might not be on speaking terms with him for a few days but you couldn't have a falling out with him.' It is doubtful if he has any lasting enemies.

The late Tom Keane, another great friend of O'Dwyer, was quoted in the book thus:

> There is nobody in the country like him for his age, or maybe … not even in the whole world, or let me go further and say, even in the next world.

I think Tom got it spot on.

7

BEHIND CLOSED DOORS

It was the Tuesday before the 2014 All-Ireland final, a beautiful September evening, and Kerry were making final preparations for the big day. The 'behind closed doors' training sessions were continuing in Fitzgerald Stadium, Killarney. Eamonn Fitzmaurice, the Kerry manager, and his back-room team were in the middle of the field issuing instructions to the panel; a full-scale mixed match was about to begin during which vital tactics would be finalised: tactics that would famously be instrumental in defeating Jim McGuinness' Donegal the following Sunday.

Then one of the Kerry back-room team heard a rustling of branches from a tree overlooking the pitch, in the grounds of St Finan's Psychiatric Hospital (now closed), which stands sentinel over the stadium. He saw what he thought was a figure of a man perched high in the branches.

One of the back-room team later told me what happened.

> Two of us left the stadium … in a couple of minutes we were under the tree and, sure enough, there he was. A man dressed in black wearing

> a cap and attempting to hide in the branches. We challenged him as to what he was up to, and he replied 'Just studying form – Kerry are a great price for the final.' It was evident from his accent that he was not a Kerryman, and sure enough it later transpired that he was from Donegal.

The incident, which was reported as 'the spy in the tree', received massive national media coverage, north and south. Was it a case of GAA espionage and the Donegal man expecting to learn aspects of the Kingdom's plans that might help his county? Whatever motives this person had, it certainly would not have happened if the training session was open to the public as had been the norm for decades, and that brings us to the thorny issue of training behind high walls and locked gates.

When the Kerry senior football manager Eamonn Fitzmaurice and the county board controversially decided in 2012 that in future the county senior footballers would hold their training sessions behind closed doors, they ended a tradition stretching back to the foundation of the GAA in the county. Attending these training sessions in Fitzgerald Stadium was always part and parcel of life for the passionate and loyal Kerry supporters.

While for many of the older followers in particular, myself included, it was a bitter blow and caused anger and disappointment, I must admit in hindsight that it was the proper decision as the game has moved into a complete new era where near-professional preparation for matches is the norm with all counties. Nevertheless it is a massive break with the county's tradition.

Eamonn Fitzmaurice is one of the best young managers in the game: his record proves this. He knows what it takes to win an All-Ireland and will do everything in his power to achieve this; he will take hard decisions where necessary. He told me: 'I understand, Weeshie, that for many a trip to Fitzgerald Stadium on a summer evening to watch the senior team is a long-standing ritual and nothing more than a social gathering to watch the players being put through their paces.' I asked him if this was the end of supporters seeing their men training for any game; he replied:

> As manager it is my job to ensure the team work in the best possible training environment but we will also have regular open training sessions to facilitate our supporters … and these will be flagged in advance on our Kerry GAA website. I have proof that scouts from other counties have attended and studied our sessions and the information that such scouting provides can make a difference. So the new arrangements are designed to provide our players with the privacy and space to develop and improve over the coming months.

Indeed, in the 2014 Munster final against favourites Cork, the strategy and team formation planned behind the locked gates was probably the main reason for Kerry's decisive win. One of the Kerry stars of that year and Footballer of the Year James O'Donoghue emphasised another aspect of the value of closed sessions:

> I think it's great, Weeshie, especially for younger players such as myself. Before when sessions were open to one and all if I was going poor in training and having a bad time the whole county would be talking about it and that would not be good for anyone's confidence. Now no matter what occurs in training no one knows anything and it makes a huge difference.

I know from years of experience that the form shown in training by every Kerry player is a topic for major debate as the watchers gather to pass on the latest news. On one occasion I was contacted by a member of the Kerry county board requesting me not to discuss on my Radio Kerry programme what was happening at the county training. Needless to say, it was not something I ever did.

When one of Kerry's greatest ever players, Declan O'Sullivan, retired in 2014 I queried him in relation to training behind closed doors. He said:

> Training behind closed doors was definitely the reason why we beat Donegal in the final. The game is gone so professional now, people are always looking for that little extra percentage. With hundreds of people attending training of course there would be people taking notes and things get out around the county and beyond.
>
> Also you will have players going at each other during training and incidents will happen as players strive their best. It's all healthy if it happens in a closed environment where fellows won't have to hear about things the following day out on the street. The tactics we used in all games was a big part of how we prepared for each team, so when training in private we felt safe in the knowledge we could surprise teams and we did.

The late Páidí Ó Sé once told me that he firmly believed scouts from other counties would regularly attend his training sessions, and that before the 2003 semi-final against Tyrone they had been monitored on a few occasions. I met people from all over the country regularly over the years; Killarney of course is a huge attraction as a holiday destination, and attending Kerry training was a recognised part of one's evening entertainment.

Attendance at training by the fanatical supporters became larger and larger as the great day approached; families arrived to Fitzgerald Stadium decked out in a blaze of green and gold, kids were in their element as they pressed their faces against the fencing surrounding the pitch, pleading with the players for autographs or photos. The excitement was infectious as the countdown continued. It was an amazing time, tradition being handed down from generation to generation.

Since I became a Kerry football fan over sixty years ago I have come to appreciate in a very deep way exactly what football means to the Kerry people, and why Kerry football fans are so knowledgeable and well informed in all things Kerry. I never cease to be amazed at what I learn from just listening to and discussing Kerry football with the most unlikely individuals. The debates that take place as one watches training can be fascinating: as you sit in the stand or on the hill you will meet the real football guru, and I guarantee you will learn your football history at these sessions if you fall in with the right people.

As I have attended Kerry training sessions since 1955, one thing has struck me forcefully, and that is the ever-evolving cycle of Kerry footballers. Indeed I have often discussed this continuing handing down of tradition with fellow watchers, and at the end of the day we agree that tradition was the one defining factor that prevailed during all those successful or barren years.

Watchers from the hill or stand whom I have been fortunate to learn from have included Murt Galvin, Jimmy Fleming and Mick Mahoney, all now gone to their eternal rewards; men whom I have spent hours with on a bitterly cold March evening as the lads were put through their paces. Indeed, memories of teams training under lights on the small pitch in Fitzgerald Stadium, on miserable winter nights when you wouldn't put the cat out, come flooding back.

A few watchers, well clothed, huddled together in some dark shadowy corner of the field as often blinding, stinging sheets of hail and rain tested the mettle of the staunchest Kerry follower: those nights were a million miles away from the pageantry and excitement of Croke Park on All-Ireland final day. But days and nights like these produce the brilliant and often unbeatable Kerry footballer. If ever the old adage was true, it is here: 'Success is 90% perspiration and 10% inspiration.'

The thousands of football followers from all over Ireland who have walked across the little practice ground in Fitzgerald Stadium to gain entrance to the main pitch would never have realised that many Kerry sides spent countless hours here building up stamina, strength and power for the assault on the championship. The late Páidí Ó Sé during his term as manager made great use of this little training pitch to knock his men into shape as they prepared for the road to glory in 1997 and 2000.

On many January and February nights you would see heavily tracksuited players slogging around and around, sending sheets of freezing cold water in their wake as they struggled to shed the winter pounds on the waterlogged surfaces. The remark 'Your man wintered well' would imply of course that a player was carrying excess body weight. The late Murt Galvin would always point out the player with the big backside as 'very unfit'. The late and lovely Kerry bagman of the fifties and sixties, Gaffney Duggan, had his own way of describing this. I often heard him remark that a player was suffering from duck's disease; when queried as to this strange affliction he answered 'Arse too close to the ground.'

Long summer and autumn evenings watching, studying and admiring the Kerry players preparing for the big championship games were special. Hundreds of fans came from far and wide to sit and enjoy the spectacle in Fitzgerald Stadium. Kerry men and women home on holidays from faraway places would be in attendance from early in the evening till the final whistle sounded and the weary players trooped off to the dressing rooms for a well-earned shower. I would meet these members of the Kerry Diaspora practically every year. Two men can be held up as typical examples.

Noel and Liam Brosnan, brothers from the town of Killarney, joined the priesthood in the early fifties; both emigrated to America, were elevated to the position of Monsignor and settled in San Antonio, Texas. Home on holidays every year before the All-Ireland semi-final, when Kerry were still in contention they would spend every evening at the stadium watching the boys in action. Autographs would be sought, photographs taken and nuggets of information gathered. It was the highlight of the year, what they had dreamed of and what they lived for. Sadly Noel has since died.

The expert watcher will cast his or her eye over the panel noting body shape, weight, running style; any sign of a limp or a man yielding to some little injury would be the subject of the greatest debate. Will such a player be fit? He was missing for the last few nights, or maybe he was togged out but just jogging around on his own. If a player goes down injured in a practice game before a big match the expert watchers will go silent or speak in hushed tones, knowing that injury is the one great fear that might upset the best-laid plans.

An injury scare will be a cause for animated debate in the local hostelries later that night and the following day, as the watchers retell to the bar-stool audiences exactly what happened. Indeed, many the man has given the impression of great medical knowledge as he described in what area of the body the injury occurred and just how serious it appeared to be.

Watching Kerry training is not entirely the domain of male followers. Women young and old are frequently to be seen studying the form, and two ladies from Gneeveguilla, just outside Killarney, are regular watchers. Treasa O'Leary and her great friend Helen O'Leary – the latter a daughter of the late, legendary box player Johnny O'Leary – are regular attendees, and boy do they know their football. Both are fit to take their place on the sideline as selectors, so vast is their knowledge of all things Kerry.

The final week before all big championship games is special; none more so than the week preceding an All-Ireland final. People seem to lose the run of themselves completely, and you will notice a distinctive change in the behaviour of the diehard supporter. Wherever you go it's football, morning, noon and night. A walk to the local newsagent for the daily paper might take hours as your opinion on the big game is eagerly sought. The waiting game is a massive part of the excitement and anticipation of Kerry being in All-Ireland senior football finals, and without this exciting build-up life might be very dull indeed.

In some ways we have become a little bit blasé about being in finals, but that can be expected in a county that is steeped in success. The old adage 'familiarity breeds contempt' might be an apt description in this instance. Having contested a total of fifty-eight senior finals, it is understandable that Kerry followers know what it's all about.

The build-up for Kerry begins immediately after the All-Ireland semi-final. Firstly the opposition is fully discussed; then begins debate about the Kerry team. Will there be changes in the starting fifteen? Is such a player injured? Will another be back from injury for the final? The possibilities and speculations are endless. And then of course there is the ongoing saga of tickets for the match, tickets for the train and even tickets for the plane.

It's surprising that some budding entrepreneur from West Kerry has not chartered a boat to bring the Kerry fans into Dublin harbour on All-Ireland final day. The schools of Kerry really get involved with their beautiful hand-drawn posters, paintings of players and images adorning the walls and windows of the classrooms around the Kingdom.

Cars are painted green and gold and flags are erected in the most desolate and difficult-to-reach places. I can vividly remember the Kerry flags blowing magnificently and proudly from the spire of St Mary's Cathedral, Killarney in 2004. Steeplejacks were working high above the ground on this beautiful cathedral and thrilled the home supporters.

Donkeys, ponies and sheep are painted in the Kingdom colours. Songs are written for the occasion. Kerry jerseys are to be seen everywhere, worn by young and old. I saw a specially knitted jersey on a three-year-old child. The word 'tradition' and the soul of Kerry football again come to mind.

I knew one lovely Killarney lady who, back in 2005, although terminally ill, insisted that her fingernails and toenails be painted in the Kerry colours: every second one green and gold, green and gold.

8

KERRY'S GREATEST RIVALS

Cork

Kerry's greatest opponents have unquestionably been Cork. Because of the provincial structure of the GAA and a seeded draw in the province, they have met in most Munster finals through the decades. Kerry have the upper hand in terms of titles won, but Cork always feel that they can beat Kerry, and Kerry are never complacent about a Cork challenge.

Nothing equals a Munster football final day in Killarney. The atmosphere is electric: green and gold, red and white through my home town. It is good-humoured; Cork supporters love making a weekend of it or taking a day out for the match. Even the legendary Cork goalkeeper/manager Billy Morgan, despite the often bitter rivalry between the counties, expressed his love of the occasion to me in an interview:

> Well, for me the Munster final in Killarney is the one you look forward to. Croke Park is great and when Cork are there on All-Ireland semi-final or final day, it is something you really look forward to, but

> the atmosphere in Killarney is extra special.
>
> On the Sunday morning you can sense this real, palpable atmosphere stirring; even the week leading up to a Munster final is exciting. There is this buzz building all the time. In my earlier days we stayed in a hotel in the centre of town; you'd go outside and there'd be hordes of Cork and Kerry supporters and they would mix with the players. You wouldn't get that now. It was something special to be part of.

Kerry's Mick O'Dwyer, who as manager and player has been involved in more Munster finals than any other person dead or alive, also spoke to me about the uniqueness of the day.

> The atmosphere on Munster final day is ahead of what you'd get on All-Ireland final day … there usually was nothing between the two counties. Had there been a loser's back-door playoff when Billy was playing and I managing Kerry, Cork and Kerry would have met in quite a number of All-Ireland finals. Cork always produced fantastic footballers. Our hardest games when we were going well in the late seventies were against Cork. That is the truth and it's wonderful to see that whoever wins or loses, supporters mingle in the hostelries and enjoy the banter after the match.

Cork star Denny Long told me one time:

> O'Dwyer used to drive the Cork lads mental when he would visit their dressing room following the usual Kerry victory. He would stand in the middle of the cramped space and repeat the very same line after

> each win over the deadly enemy: 'There is no doubt about it, lads, but ye are the second best team in the whole of Ireland.' We were pig sick of listing to that bullshit every year.

Since the introduction of the open draw in 2000, Kerry and Cork have met even more frequently. An extremely talented Cork team emerged in the first decade of this century, but this coincided with the arrival of a superb Kerry team which won five All-Irelands between 2000 and 2009 and contested six finals in a row. Cork could beat Kerry on occasions in Munster but proved incapable of doing so in Croke Park. They met in two All-Ireland finals, 2007 and 2009, and four semi-finals. One semi-final was drawn, but Kerry won the replay and all other matches. When Kerry's run came to an end and Cork won the 2010 final, most Kerry followers were glad for them but determined to put them back in their box in 2011.

The greatest game of football I ever saw was the Munster final replay of 1976. It went to extra time and was packed with incidents. The atmosphere was amazing – I will never forget it – and one man sitting near me collapsed and was rushed to hospital. That victory was a turning point in Kerry's fortunes. Cork had an excellent team at the time. Had they got through that day, they and not Kerry would have dominated the next few years.

There were more than a few debatable decisions in that magnificent encounter. With Cork a good bit ahead, Mikey Sheehy kicked a short free to Seanie Walsh, whose bullet of a shot was saved on the line by Cork defender Brian Murphy. The umpire proceeded to raise the green flag: wrong decision, in my opinion. The amazing thing about that incident, and it has stayed with me to this day, is the fact that the Cork players never protested.

Then Declan Barron scored what I believed to be a marvellous goal when he rose and punched to the Kerry net. That was disallowed: Declan was adjudged to have been in the square. Wrong decision also, in my opinion.

On 24 July 1955 I saw the green and gold in action for the first time as Kerry beat Cork in sweltering conditions in Killarney, 0–14 to 2–6. 45,000 supporters crammed Fitzgerald Stadium that memorable day. The terrace was black with people packed together like sardines. No such slogan as health and safety, and not a safety barrier to be seen. Even the boundary wall served as a vantage point, and it was from here on high that I viewed my first Munster final. Memories of that day are of some superb long-range points lofted over by Paudie Sheehy and Tadhgie Lyne. The following year, 1956, I saw Kerry lose a game for the first time when, in a replay in Killarney, a last-minute point for Cork by Army Captain Niall Fitzgerald stopped the Kingdom's drive for victory.

There have been magnificent games between the counties and of course some disappointing clashes, but the weeks leading up to a Munster final never disappoint. I have been fortunate to have seen some of the Rebel County's greatest players down through the decades: Dinny Allen, Declan Barron, Paddy O'Driscoll, Dan Murray, Denis Bernard, Toots Kelliher, Kevin Jer O'Sullivan, Denny Long, John Coleman, Ray Cummins, Colman Corrigan, Dave Barry, Niall Cahalane, Jimmy Barry-Murphy, Colin Corkery, Larry Tompkins, Teddy McCarthy and of course Billy Morgan, the greatest of all.

I have been hooked on Munster finals since that year long ago, and when the teams race onto the field, the wonderful expectations of what we are about to witness never wane. Whether in Cork or Killarney, the pulse quickens and the heart rate soars. In 1973 I was present when Cork hammered Kerry 5–12 to 1–15; I vividly recall, as Kerry fans were streaming from the stadium well before the final whistle, Cork fans jumping up from their seats and shouting, 'Lock the fucking gates and keep them in; they have seen us suffering long enough!'

Following the 2007 All-Ireland final against Cork, which Kerry won, I gained entry to the Kerry dressing room and secured an interview with Paul Galvin. He sat in the corner, seemingly oblivious to the sight of the gleaming silver Sam Maguire Cup standing on the table before him. Reporters and photographers were scurrying around, anxious to secure a precious interview with a member of the newly crowned All-Ireland champions. Galvin had seen all before. It appeared to me that for him it was just a case of another job done and dusted. The old enemy had been kept down for another year, so move on and prepare for the next battle. But the importance of the victory summed up for me the deadly rivalry between the two counties. This, then, was what it all boiled down to: very close to a matter of life and death.

So how did Galvin feel following that historic win over the old enemy?

> It's a fantastic feeling, Weeshie: there was so much riding on this game for Kerry due to the fact that it was Cork in an All-Ireland final. I felt that everything we had achieved and everything that Kerry football stood for was on the line to day.

'Was it really that serious?', I asked.

> Without a doubt, I felt that 100 years or more of being the greatest county in Gaelic football and dominating Cork for so long that if they had beaten us today we wouldn't have been allowed back into the county in my opinion. The stakes were that big for us, our reputations and our pride in Kerry football was riding on seventy minutes: that's how I looked on it.

Kerry v. Cork: a magnificent, never-ending saga.

Dublin

Dublin and Kerry are polar opposites, and the natural city v. country binary ensures an enduring rivalry. In the blue corner, Dublin are the city team, with fanatical supporters who follow them to every corner of Ireland. In the green and gold corner are Kerry, the rural champions – 'culchies' in the vernacular – playing 'the Jacks', as the Dubs are dubbed. Always at stake is county pride, but also something deeper for Ireland. This is the greatest rivalry of Gaelic football and possibly of Irish sport as a whole.

Between them, Kerry and Dublin have won sixty-two of the 127 All-Irelands ever contested, and in eighty-three All-Ireland senior finals at least one of the two counties has been involved. They are way out in front on the role of honour, Kerry with thirty-seven titles and Dublin with twenty-five.

Mere numbers don't tell the whole story. Dublin v. Kerry seems the essence of Gaelic football. The glamour of their meetings in the 1970s crystallised the sport in the television age. It could even date back well before my time, to the Laune Rangers–Young Irelands 1892 final, played in 1893, when the Killorglin team felt very aggrieved at their treatment at the hands of the referee and the Dublin supporters.

But the modern rivalry began in 1955 when an unfancied Kerry team, playing the supposedly outdated catch-and-kick style, conquered a stylish Dublin side led by Kevin Heffernan, who were widely expected to end a twenty-one-year wait for a championship win. The Kingdom's victory cast a long shadow on Dublin GAA, and Heffernan was driven to avenge it for the rest of his life.

The 1959 and 1962 semi-finals, which I attended, were memorable matches. Mick O'Connell was at his most majestic at midfield and Dublin, I believe, were his favourite opponents. I am convinced that Croke Park championship matches and Dublin bring the very best out of great players, and in that semi-final of 1962, which Kerry won, I was privileged to see one of those great moments in Kerry football.

Back then, sideline balls were kicked off the ground, not from the hands as we see in today's game. In the first half a sideline ball was awarded to Kerry thirty-five yards out from the Dublin goal, on the left under the Hogan Stand where I was sitting. Mick O'Connell placed the ball, stood back and, aided by a very slight breeze, curled the ball over the crossbar for a beautiful point.

Even better was to follow in the second half, and once more it was O'Connell showing his magnificent kicking skills. Again it happened in front of the Hogan Stand, now forty-five yards from goal: another sideline kick, this time into the wind. It would need deadly accuracy, supreme concentration and a powerful kick. The massive crowd were hushed in anticipation.

The Island man was unerring; the ball sailed cleanly through the posts for one of the greatest kicks I have ever seen. The massive crowd in the stand – both the Kerry and Dublin supporters – rose in thunderous applause. Kerry–Dublin bringing out all that is great and good in our game.

The most notable period of rivalry occurred between 1974 and 1986, when great teams emerged from both counties. Of the thirteen All-Irelands in those years, Kerry won eight and Dublin four. The thirteenth, in 1982, was won by Offaly when Seamus Darby's last-minute goal deprived the greatest team of all time of a historic five-in-a-row, as described elsewhere in this book.

Kerry and Dublin met in six finals and one semi-final during those years. Kerry won five finals, lost one, and lost the famous 1977 semi-final. Players from the two teams have remained on very friendly terms through the decades. There was no meeting in a final between 1985 and 2011: Kerry won some semi- and quarter-finals. In recent years the rivalry has re-emerged: two finals and one semi-final, all won by Dublin.

The tables have been turned, but they will turn again. For many, the meeting of Dublin and Kerry represents the definitive September showdown and a reminder of some classic encounters that gripped the nation

Kerry 0–12, Dublin 1–6: 1955 All-Ireland final

I was among the 87,102 crammed into Croke Park – then a record attendance for a final. It was my first trip to headquarters, and this unforgettable encounter defined my life in relation to football. Kerry were deserving winners, but they had to withstand late pressure from the Dubs, who found renewed momentum after Ollie Freeney's goal five minutes from time. Heroic defending from the Kingdom's Jerome O'Shea, Sean Murphy, John Cronin and Micksie Palmer in those dying moments kept Dublin at bay.

My Killarney Legion clubmate Johnny Culloty, just gone eighteen years of age, was one of Kerry's corner-forwards. Tadghie Lyne was top scorer for the victors with 0–6. Kevin Heffernan lined out at full-forward for Dublin. He was one of the greatest players of his generation and would win an All-Ireland medal in 1958, but he had to wait until he was Dublin manager before he would get one over on Kerry in an All-Ireland final.

Kerry 2–12, Dublin 0–11: 1975 All-Ireland final

It was a case of 'all quiet on the Hill' as Kerry's young guns comfortably defeated the reigning All-Ireland champions by seven points. In his first season in charge, Mick O'Dwyer masterminded a terrific victory as Kerry's speed of thought in testing conditions proved too much for Heffo's Dubs. Kerry were the youngest side ever to leave the county, and probably the most loved team of all.

At half-time O'Dwyer's troops led by 1–6 to 0–4, with the late John Egan getting the goal after three minutes. Jimmy Keaveney points from placed balls kept the Dubs in touch to some degree in the second half, but the Green and Gold always had an extra gear and a Ger O'Driscoll goal and a Pat Spillane point sealed the county's twenty-third All-Ireland title.

The only downside for the victors was the bad injury picked up by their captain Mickey Ned O'Sullivan after twenty minutes when he became the meat in a Dublin sandwich as he bore down on the Canal End goal. The Kenmare man woke up in hospital, as I describe in a later chapter, and his Kenmare teammate Pat Spillane accepted the Sam Maguire Cup.

Dublin 3–12, Kerry 1–13: 1977 All-Ireland semi-final

This was, in my view, one of the fastest-moving games in decades. Kerry were a goal to the good at the break – their green flag coming from Sean Walsh – after a period in which the victors hit eight wides. However, Dublin's dominance of midfield in the second half and Bernard Brogan's introduction in that sector saw Heffo's men gain a foothold. John McCarthy goaled shortly after the break to bring the sides level. Points were exchanged thereafter as the intensity increased, but the Dubs' graph was rising faster.

In a dramatic finale, after a move started by Brian Mullins, the ball found its way to Tony Hanahoe, who slipped it to David Hickey; he shot brilliantly to the back of the net. Hickey, Hanahoe and Bobby Doyle combined to set up Bernard Brogan for the clinching score as Dublin ran out five-point winners. They would win a third All-Ireland in four years by beating Armagh in the decider.

Kerry 5–11, Dublin 0–9: 1978 All-Ireland final

This game will be most remembered for Mikey Sheehy's goal that caught out

Dublin custodian Paddy Cullen, as I describe in a later chapter. On a gloomy, wet day at GAA HQ, Kerry's brilliance simply destroyed Dublin. The Dubs started brightly, but the force was with the Munster men. Sheehy's opportunism was sandwiched between John Egan's opening goal and a hat-trick of green flags for Eoin 'Bomber' Liston. The big full-forward from the Beal club in Ballybunion was a vital part of Mick O'Dwyer's magnificent side, and his three goals in the rain that day are forever spoken about in the Kingdom. Kerry's winning margin was seventeen points. No team has managed to eclipse that margin since.

Kerry 1–14, Dublin 2–11: 2001 All-Ireland quarter-final

Both sides celebrated at the final whistle at Tipperary's Semple Stadium after an absorbing tussle. For long stages it looked like the Kingdom would reign, even though Dublin would rue goal chances that Collie Moran and Dessie Farrell spurned in the first half. After 46 minutes, the Green and Gold were eight points clear. Surely no way back for the Dubs!

When referee Michael Curley, a Garda Superintendent, awarded Kerry a somewhat dubious free, Dublin manager Tom Carr remonstrated strongly with the Galway official. That face-off brought Carr's side to life. Vinny Murphy and Darren Homan bagged quick-fire goals. Deep into injury time, the Leinster side were ahead by a point.

The mercurial Maurice Fitzgerald was introduced late on and would prove to be the Kerry saviour. His point from forty-five metres out on the sideline in the dying minutes of the game was superbly executed via the outside of his right boot. I was in the direct line of the flight of the ball in my position high up in Radio Kerry's commentary spot, and it was the greatest point kicked under enormous pressure I have ever seen. The game finished in a draw.

Kerry would make good use of the lifeline thrown by Fitzgerald with a relatively comfortable 2–12 to 1–12 win over their arch-rivals in the replay at Semple Stadium one week later.

Kerry 1–24, Dublin 1–7: 2009 All-Ireland quarter-final

Dublin were simply demolished in front of a crowd of 81,890 by a Kingdom outfit bursting with energy, style and substance. Colm Cooper's goal after just forty seconds set the tone for Kerry supremacy, and they led by 1–14 to 0–3 at the break, with Gooch hitting 1–4 and skipper Darren O'Sullivan three points. Conal Keaney netted a Dublin goal on fifty-six minutes, but Kerry responded with the last five points of the game to win by a massive seventeen-point margin, Cooper finishing with a 1–7 tally.

Jack O'Connor's side made a mockery of the underdog status they had been saddled with in the build-up to the game. After losing the Munster final replay to Cork, Kerry stumbled through the qualifiers and narrowly avoided embarrassing defeat against Longford, Sligo and Antrim. The talk was that they were in disarray and the Dubs were on the rise.

But give Kerry a fitting stage – give them Dublin as opponents and the wide open spaces of Croke Park – and the magic returns. 'We felt that we worked very hard over the last couple of weeks since the Cork game and that somewhere along the line that we would click', Kerry manager Jack O'Connor told me after their truly memorable display: as great as I have ever seen from a Kerry team against the Dubs.

Kerry could do nothing wrong, their champagne football ending in a succession of spectacular points. Defenders Tom O'Sullivan and Tomás Ó Sé (2) got on the score sheet, and it was clear that this was not to be Dublin's day when Alan Brogan (via goalkeeper Diarmuid Murphy's fingertips) and Diarmuid

Connolly both smashed the ball against the crossbar. Bizarrely, Dublin manager Pat Gilroy told reporters after the rout that his players 'were like startled earwigs'. Kerry went on to claim their thirty-sixth All Ireland title, beating Cork in the final 0–16 to 1–9.

Another riveting performance, and once again I was in such a privileged position as analyst for Radio Kerry, broadcasting the match to emigrants all over the world on the Internet and to everyone at home in Ireland. How lucky can you get? One man emailed me the following week from Australia telling me that he had been sitting around a camp fire somewhere near Wagga Wagga, listening the game on Radio Kerry on his iPhone. 'I was in the company of a group of Aborigines, Weeshie,' he wrote, 'but they hadn't a clue what you were saying; the Kerry accent baffled them.'

Dublin 1–12, Kerry 1–11: 2011 All-Ireland final

There was heartbreak for the Kingdom as goalkeeper Stephen Cluxton converted a free in stoppage time to give Dublin their first All-Ireland Senior Football Championship title since 1995. Colm Cooper slotted home a superb nineteenth-minute goal, but two points each from the Brogan brothers helped Dublin to a 0–6 to 1–2 interval lead.

Kerry, managed by one of their great leaders, Jack O'Connor, were four points ahead before substitute Kevin McManamon scored a sixty-fourth-minute goal for Dublin. And in a gripping finish that encapsulated all that is special about Kerry–Dublin games, Barry John Keane was in my opinion wrongly penalised by the referee. Cluxton kept his cool to make history as the first goalkeeper to score an All-Ireland final winner. 'The Jacks are back', roared the banner on Hill 16, and Pat Gilroy's side finally emerged from the shadows to revisit the Promised Land.

Dublin 3–18, Kerry 3–11: 2013 All-Ireland semi-final

Late goals from Kevin McManamon and Eoghan O'Gara won an epic All-Ireland SFC semi-final for Dublin as they fended off Kerry by seven points. Kerry stunned the Dubs with three first-half goals, from James O'Donoghue (2, 1 penalty) and Donnchadh Walsh. Paul Mannion netted for Dublin, but they trailed by 3–5 to 1–9 at the break.

Both sides had spells of dominance in the second half, but McManamon scored a brilliant solo goal in the seventieth minute, followed by an O'Gara strike in stoppage time that sealed it.

Dublin 0–12, Kerry 0–9: 2015 All-Ireland final

Once again I was on Radio Kerry duty for the meeting of these giants of the game. Questions are still being asked in Kerry in relation to the selection of the team. Captain Kieran Donaghy was dramatically dropped from the starting fifteen and was introduced, too late, as a substitute; big Tommy Walsh, home from Australia, saw no action and the terrible conditions would probably have suited him.

Paul Galvin, who had retired the previous year, was controversially brought on as a sub; James O'Donoghue and Paul Geaney, who scored five points between them, were taken off in the second half.

Dublin have a reputation of prevailing in adverse conditions, and we saw them give a superb team effort from one to fifteen as they overpowered Kerry. Indeed, a seven- or eight-point victory would have been a more realistic reflection of the play. And Dublin's brilliant defending impressed me more than anything else.

Their discipline in tackling without conceding scorable frees was unbelievable: the fact that Kerry scored just one free – from close in, late in the game from Brian Sheehan – tells the whole story. Was it the first time in history that Kerry raised just one white flag from frees?

Of course the conditions played a huge part in making this a disappointing spectacle, but they were the same for both teams. It was a day for stronger men; conditions should have been the foremost topic of debate among the selectors after just fifteen minutes. This was a very poor Kerry display and they were always chasing the game. They looked out of sorts, disjointed, lacking the freshness and spring in their step so necessary to achieve victory.

Kieran Donaghy and Darren O'Sullivan added drive and spirit when introduced; they had the necessary strength and experience which was obvious. Tommy Walsh, I feel, should also have been thrown into the fray, while it is strange that Marc Ó Sé was listed as number eighteen: as we now know, he was unable to play.

Another strange decision was the withdrawing of James O'Donoghue: he had failed, like others, to win possession at times in the dreadful conditions but kicked three points and set up two more. Being a recognised goal scorer, he was always capable of finding the net.

I thought Kieran Donaghy should have a had a penalty for the second tackle committed on him in the square, and while Killian Young will be remembered for failing to collect a ball close to goal when a score looked on, it must be remembered that a defender seldom finds himself in these situations and may not be sharp enough to take advantage as a recognised forward would. The better team won on the day, but no fault to Brendan Kealy, Shane Enright, Jonathan Lyne, Darren O'Sullivan, Donnchadh Walsh and Kieran Donaghy, who were excellent in the conditions.

Tyrone

Although Kerry and Tyrone met for the first time in the championship in 1986, the rivalry between the counties is intense. In the first fifteen years of this century Mickey Harte and his Tyrone men got under the skin of Kerry footballers and supporters by deploying tactics that were both innovative and controversial.

This reminds me of something I have written about in Chapter 3: the arrival of another Northern side, Down, back in the sixties. They changed the thinking and philosophy of Kerry football. Tyrone's victories in 2003, 2005 and 2008 also challenged Kerry's traditional values and changed the way the Kingdom approached the game.

Jack O'Connor, one of Kerry's most successful managers, summed it up best in his book *Keys to the Kingdom*:

> Losing to Tyrone is worse than losing to almost anyone else. Not that there is much history between us, that's the point. There's arrogance to Northern football which rubs Kerry people up the wrong way. They're flash and nouveau riche and full of it. Northern teams advertise themselves well. They talk about how they did it, they go on and on about this theory and that practice as if they'd just split the atom. They build up a mythology about themselves that doesn't sit well in Kerry.

Strong words from, the South Kerry man, and he's spot-on.

The 1986 All-Ireland final was as dramatic a game as I have seen. It was the swansong of the greatest Kerry side of all time, and they stole that final from Tyrone.

There was a massive build-up to this game, and the comment I most recall came from Tyrone full-forward Damian O'Hagan, who said that he wanted to win an All-Ireland 'for the boys in Long Kesh'. Mick O'Dwyer marked his tenth All-Ireland final as a manager; he had played on ten occasions. Truly a phenomenal record.

All those years ago I watched from the Hogan Stand, my young son Kieran sitting on my lap. It was a game that had everything: tremendous atmosphere, Tyrone the underdogs playing out of their skins, the promise for three-quarters of an hour of a massive upset and Kerry at the end only just surviving.

After ten minutes of the second half Tyrone led their illustrious opponents by seven points, 1–8 to 0–4. Then Kevin McCabe failed to goal from a penalty: this was crucial in the final analysis. The old firm of Pat Spillane and Mikey Sheehy scored a goal each and Kerry raced away in the final minutes to a 2–15 to 1–10 victory. It marked the finish of this great side, and when the counties met again in the 2003 All Ireland semi-final everything would have changed.

In 2003 I was positioned high in the Michael O'Hehir media centre of the Hogan Stand, again in the privileged position of Radio Kerry match analyst. A dramatic passage of play was about to unfold before the eyes of thousands of supporters in Croke Park and the massive television audience. It came to define that Tyrone team.

First Dara Ó Cinnéide, then Eoin Brosnan, and finally Darragh Ó Sé tried to carry the ball forward for Kerry. On each occasion they were surrounded and driven back by a swarm of Tyrone players that tore into them like a pack of wolves.

A photograph of the moment that Brosnan was knocked to his knees – with eight Tyrone men around him, manager Mickey Harte looking on from the sideline and not a Kerry teammate in sight – became iconic. I had never seen anything like it in all my years watching the game and I was stunned at the ferocity of the Tyrone men. It did not just sum up Tyrone's superiority on the day. It was the moment that symbolised the rabid intensity that drove them to three All-Ireland titles in the noughties. The Northern men won that game 0–13 to 0–6 and went on to defeat Armagh in the final.

A bitter rivalry had been born. Pat Spillane, analyst on *The Sunday Game*, added fuel to the fire when he described the Tyrone style of play as 'puke football'. This caused outrage in Tyrone and has entered GAA folklore.

The two sides met again in the 2005 final, when a truly absorbing game saw Tyrone hold their nerve to claim a second All-Ireland title and deny Kerry back-to-back titles. A Dara Ó Cinnéide goal after seven minutes had the Kingdom on the front foot, and the early exchanges saw Colm Cooper kick some fine scores. The Gooch took a heavy knock to the face at the Canal End of Croke Park in an incident that annoyed the Kerry supporters and inflamed passions. No action was taken, however.

Tyrone took control of the game in the second quarter and outscored their rivals by 1–5 to 0–2. Brian McGuigan, Brian Dooher and Ryan Mellon were exerting more of an influence in the half-forward line, and just before half-time the Red Hand struck for a crucial goal at the Railway End of Croke Park. Owen Mulligan fed Peter Canavan and the latter's deft ground shot beat goalkeeper Diarmuid Murphy and found the corner of the net. It was a magnificent score.

Canavan was withdrawn at the break; his reappearance after fifty-five minutes gave Tyrone a psychological boost and served to quell a Kingdom comeback in the shape of a Tomás Ó Sé goal. That left a point between the sides. Mickey Harte's men, with Seán Cavanagh now more of a threat in the middle, showed the greater composure to see the game out by three points.

This was a great Tyrone side – no doubt about that, their wins proved it –

but there was a cynical side to their game. A memory I have of that 2005 game is of Peter Canavan, a wonderful player, resorting to pulling Colm Cooper to the ground as Kerry launched one last attack. Cooper gave a pass, ran for the return and was hauled to the ground – no free. Kerry were still learning; Tyrone proved once again their masters in tactical awareness.

Manager Jack O'Connor took the defeat very hard. Always a great person to interview, he made it clear to me that Kerry football would have to change. As in 2003, Tyrone had completely out-tackled Kerry, turning over the ball on a regular basis. So the Kerry style of tackling changed. A new level of physicality was born: new drills, highly competitive games in training, an emphasis on tackling the player with the ball and having players breaking past heavy tackles. Just like Down and Galway in the sixties, Tyrone was influencing Kerry's approach to the game.

The rivalry intensified in 2008. Kerry had regained the Sam Maguire in 2006 and, under new management, retained it in the following year. When they qualified to meet Tyrone in the 2008 final, there was an expectation in the county that this great team would achieve three-in-a-row; to do it at the expense of Tyrone would balance the history books.

It was a final tinged with emotion for Tyrone, following the death on the night before the game of their goalkeeper John Devine's father. Devine's place in goal was taken by big Pascal McConnell, who had a great game and made a brilliant late save. Declan O'Sullivan was one-on-one with the goalkeeper at the Railway End, but McConnell spread himself to deny Kerry the winning score.

Kerry were dominant in the first half but led by only a point at half-time. The so-called twin towers strategy, featuring Kieran Donaghy and Tommy Walsh in the full-forward line, was nullified by Mickey Harte's placing of both McMahon brothers in the full-back line. Kerry didn't seem to have another strategy, and a Tyrone goal from the second half throw-in left them chasing the game, as in 2005. They fought back to take the lead at one stage but Tyrone soon equalised, and pulled away with points in the final minutes. It finished 1–15 to 0–14. Manager Pat O'Shea, who had guided Kerry to the previous year's All-Ireland final victory over Cork, stepped down in October following the Tyrone defeat.

This had been Kerry's best chance of a championship victory over Tyrone. In 2003 Tyrone were clearly superior, in 2005 marginally superior, but this match could have gone either way. Kerry supporters were sore at losing an All-Ireland that could have been won, at losing the three-in-a-row, and especially at losing to Tyrone.

I sensed the mood in the county following this latest defeat by Mickey Harte's men as dark and angry, but the Northern tactics, preparation and performance on the day must be greatly admired. To have yet another big championship win over the Kingdom was a magnificent achievement for Tyrone's manager Mickey Harte, one of my favourite people.

Kerry and Tyrone met again at Fitzgerald Stadium, Killarney, on 22 July 2012 in the All-Ireland qualifiers. It was one of those never-to-be-forgotten days of my football life as over 24,000 supporters gathered for the latest instalment of the now bitter rivalry. Once again this championship meeting was as fiery as they come, ending with sixteen yellow cards and one red card as referee David Coldrick struggled to keep order. But this was a Tyrone team in swift decline; they were no match for a fired-up Kerry side, and the Kingdom finally beat Tyrone in a championship match, 1–16 to 1–6. When the final whistle sounded the result was greeted with tears of joy by some players and wild scenes of euphoria among supporters. No sleeping dogs are ever left to lie when these deadly rivals meet.

An emotional Paul Galvin, the man of the match, paid tribute to his teammates in a post-match interview. His passion showed just how deeply the three previous championship defeats to Tyrone had affected the Kerry players. The Finuge native hit back at the critics who had been writing obituaries for this Kerry side after some poor performances during the summer:

> What do you say about this Kerry team? They're great men. A lot of the talk during the week, writing this team off, served only to fuel the great men in that dressing room. We've been carrying a lot of hurt for the last nine or ten years; we're Kerry at the end of the day and we've suffered a few heavy defeats, a few last-minute defeats. There has been a lot written about this team and a lot of it has been disrespectful. I think today the great men in this team stood up. I'm very proud of that.

Following his retirement Galvin wrote in his book *In My Own Words*:

> to me it was more than a qualifier, to me this was an All-Ireland final, the atmosphere in Killarney was thick with tradition, one of those days when the ghosts of Kerry's past came out to play with us. The Kerry supporters came out to play too. They were loud and proud.

For me the most abiding memory of that July day in Killarney is the emotion and feeling shown to Tyrone manager Mickey Harte following the game. His family were still reeling following the traumatic trial in Mauritius where two men were found not guilty of murdering the long-serving Tyrone boss's daughter, the beautiful Michaela, on her honeymoon on the tropical island. His team were well beaten on the field, their intense rivalry with Kerry was still intact, but the oft-touted bond between the wider GAA family was on display in Fitzgerald that Saturday night.

I had conducted a series of after-match interviews and was outside the dressing room area when Mickey Harte emerged. A huge crowd of Kerry supporters had congregated to applaud their players, but it was the genial Tyrone manager they turned to. It began with a ripple of applause and then built up to a loud, prolonged ovation: it got louder and louder and I, like many others, was deeply moved by the grace and dignity of this man who had lost his beloved daughter in such tragic circumstances. As the Tyrone players boarded the bus the applause continued, and even people on the streets of Killarney clapped as the bus passed by.

If you wanted your faith in decency and respect restored, then Killarney at about eight o'clock that Saturday evening was the place to be. In the overall context, the result of the game was irrelevant for me on this poignant occasion. Kerry failed to go on and win the All-Ireland, losing to Donegal in the quarter-final 1–12 to 1–10.

Kerry and Tyrone would meet again in the All-Ireland semi-final of 2015. I interviewed Kerry boss Eamonn Fitzmaurice for Radio Kerry before the game, and he played down the significance of the games from the previous decade:

> There was a ferocious rivalry in the noughties and Tyrone had the upper hand, beating us fair and square in 2003, '05 and '08. We got some measure of revenge in 2012 when we beat them in the qualifiers in Killarney. Since then there's been a lot of change on the two new teams that will take to the pitch on Sunday. As a manager, my experience of Tyrone has been the few league games we've played.

We witnessed a fascinating, absorbing game. The introduction of Paul Geaney at half-time changed the style of the Kerry attack, similarly to the change we saw in the replayed Munster final. Colm Cooper, who had spent the first half close to the Tyrone goal and had been swallowed up by defenders, moved outfield more and his combination with James O'Donoghue and the other forwards from outside was crucial. Brendan Kealy's brilliant save from Mark Bradley's forty-fourth-minute bullet of a shot was probably the defining moment. The Kilcummin man's reactions were razor sharp. This and his brilliant second-half stop in the Munster final sent Kerry on their winning way. Kerry won by 0–18 to 1–11.

Now the Tyrone itch had been scratched – end of story? Not by a long shot – not until Kerry meet and beat Tyrone in an All-Ireland final. Many Kerry experts will say that as long as Mickey Harte is manager he will always pull some rabbit out of the hat to defeat their deadly rivals in the final. Only time will tell.

While defeating Tyrone in that 2015 semi-final left a warm glow in Kerry hearts, it was a case of out of the frying pan, into the fire as their other great rivals Dublin awaited in the final, and plunged the county into a winter of despair by winning 0–12 to 0–9.

This might not be admitted by some, but – like the Down defeats of the sixties and later – whenever the faithful Kerry followers come together to talk football, Tyrone is invariably a topic.

9

KERRY CAPTAINS: THE AGONY AND THE ECSTASY

To captain Kerry to All-Ireland glory is the most cherished honour any Kerry footballer can aspire to. Of the thousands of players who have worn the green and gold since the first Kerry team took to the field way back in the nineteenth century, only thirty-seven men have achieved that great distinction. The man who is fortunate to lead his county to victory writes himself into history's pages for evermore.

The name of every winning Kerry captain is ingrained in the memories of most Kingdom followers, and all over Kerry photographs of those captains – some old and faded – are to be seen adorning the walls of public houses, homes, hotels and club houses. It's all part of the secret of Kerry and the handing down of tradition.

However, as I have alluded to already, the captaincy has raised lots of debates and controversy down the years. Each year the Kerry captain is nominated by the team that wins the senior county championship, but this system – which continues at the request of the clubs of the county – has caused endless problems. Kerry and Cork are the only two counties in Ireland that have divisional teams contesting their premier competition.

Kerry have nine divisional sides made up of different numbers of clubs, so if one of these sides win the championship – which has happened on twenty-four occasions since 1970 – the winning club from the division nominates the captain. They might not have a man from their club on the Kerry panel, so they appoint who they believe is the best person to lead the county. This often leads to problems.

Joe Barrett and Con Brosnan (1929–32)

Indeed, problems in relation to the Kerry captaincy were occurring as far back as 1931, and the dramatic events of that year emphasise for me the uniqueness and beauty of Kerry football. Tralee side Austin Stacks won the championship in 1930, so they had the nomination for the following year. The great Joe Barrett, a winning captain in 1929 and winner of six All-Ireland medals and eight Munster Championship medals, was again appointed Kerry skipper for 1931. Barrett was a man of huge principle and great courage, and there was uproar in his club when he announced that he was handing over the captaincy to Moyvane's Con Brosnan.

The Tralee club was known for its strong Republican values. The fact that Con Brosnan had been a Free State Army Captain and Stacks' own hero Joe Barrett had handed over the captaincy to Brosnan caused a furore in the club. The two other Tralee clubs, John Mitchels and O'Rahillys, also felt that the captaincy should have gone to a Tralee man. Joe Barrett, however, was not to be swayed: he stuck to his decision, and Con Brosnan went on to lead Kerry to All-Ireland victory. It was a wonderfully magnanimous gesture by Barrett, who captained Kerry to victory for a second time in 1932.

Jas Murphy (1953)

Jas Murphy is Kerry's oldest surviving winning captain. Now in his ninety-fourth year, Jas – one of my favourite Kerry footballers – lifted the Sam Maguire in 1953 when Armagh were defeated in a dramatic game. We have often discussed the dramatic circumstances in which he was appointed captain for the final. Even now, all these years later, his memories of that year are crystal clear. It was another highly controversial and remarkable episode in Kerry football.

John Joe Sheehy was one of the five Kerry selectors who sat down to pick the team in the now demolished Park Place Hotel, Killarney for that 1953 final. His son, the late Paudie, had been a regular on the team all year and in the three championship games played was Kerry's top scorer with 3–6. When Paudie's position came up for discussion, John Joe left the room as a matter of courtesy; when he returned he was informed that his son had been dropped from the team. It caused huge controversy around the county, and of course Paudie's omission meant that a new captain had to be named for the final.

Jas heard about his appointment the following day. 'A few of us were walking down the street in Killarney when somebody came up to me and said "Congratulations!" It was news to me and it was the first I heard that Paudie was dropped. I felt for him, as we were great friends from boyhood days. Kerry brought on one sub in the final and it was not Paudie, and I always felt the selectors should have given him a run during the game.'

Jas was adamant that being captain of that Kerry team played a huge part in his life. 'I was captain for just one game and I have always felt so proud of that achievement. Everywhere I went I was introduced as the "winning captain of 1953". I am convinced it helped me greatly in my life as a member of the Garda Síochána in Cork and it was great for my club, Kerins O'Rahillys.' In his retirement Jas was made President of the great Nemo Rangers club in Cork, a distinct honour for a Kerryman. 'Invitations to events were regular and callers to the house would always want to discuss that year', he told me.

Years later, then retired, he explained to me in his home in Cork:

> Well, Weeshie, as usual a few of us adjourned to a pub to celebrate with supporters. We forgot about the time and missed the train bringing the team back home. The cup was gone and I was left behind. Paddy Bawn Brosnan and Micksie Palmer were also with me. Lucky enough we were able to get the next train out of Dublin and got into Killarney as the lads were being paraded through the town.

I had often wondered, when looking at photographs of Jackie Lyne being shouldered with the cup that year at Killarney railway station, why it was not the captain, Jas. He added in our interview: 'I was delighted that Jackie Lyne had the honor of bringing the cup through the streets of his home town Killarney as he had given wonderful service to Kerry.' A very gracious statement by an exemplary man.

Mick O'Connell (1959)

Kerry have won thirty-seven senior All-Irelands, and it's sobering to realise that of all the great Kerry players down through the decades, just twenty-five have had the privilege of accepting the Sam Maguire Cup since it was first presented in 1928. Mick O'Connell was one of these, in 1959, and no man deserved it more. That year the team won every available honour: Championship, National League and the St Brendan's Cup.

In 1958 Kerry had reached the All-Ireland semi-final, where surprise packet Derry, led by their brilliant midfielder Jim McKeever, awaited them. I watched that game from under the Cusack Stand in Croke Park; in a torrential downpour the Northern men shocked the Kingdom as they won 2–6 to 2–5. Despite the loss, this game was historic for the fact that a young Valentia Island lad named Mick O'Connell played his first championship game in Croke Park. It was the beginning of a magnificent career that would stretch to 1973.

O'Connell won his first All-Ireland in 1959; he was captain of the Kerry team that defeated Galway. A legend was born as he accepted the Sam Maguire Cup, said the obligatory few words, was cheered across the field – and left the cup behind him in the dressing room!

He was then twenty-two years old, lived on Valentia Island and rowed to the mainland before every match. He would travel to the game, play and return to the island the same day, often rowing home in darkness. No wonder he became a romantic figure who intrigued the nation. A shy, almost reclusive figure back then who gave very few interviews, O'Connell's talking was done on the pitch.

He was a pure footballer for whom cups and medals held little interest. To see Mick O'Connell at his very best was to see poetry in motion. I have seen none better to leap for a high ball and win possession cleanly in the air. I have seen none better to take frees, foot pass with deadly accuracy and swerve and dance around opponents while in possession. O'Connell possessed all the arts. I have never seen a more perfect footballer. I consider myself privileged to have seen him throughout his career with Valentia, South Kerry, Munster and Kerry. I have played with him and against him, and had the unforgettable privilege of training with him when a member of the Kerry All-Ireland winning panel of 1969.

Mick had a natural spring so that with just a few steps in his run-up, he could leap into the air, soaring high above all others, to catch the ball. With the ball in his hands, he was a master distributor. 'I was waiting under a dropping ball with Phil Stuart of Derry when I caught a glimpse of a pair of knees above my shoulder and hands gripping the ball. It was Mick O'Connell.' I quote there from his long-time midfield partner, the late Seamus Murphy. Equally adept with left or right foot, O'Connell would send the ball unerringly to a forward better positioned than himself.

Mick O'Connell's position in the history of Gaelic football is unchallenged. He was selected at centre-field on the Team of the Century and the Team of the Millennium. While attempting to adjudicate on who was the greatest footballer of all is a futile exercise, all I can say is that I have seen them all – Kerry and non-Kerry – since 1955, and I have never seen a player who was the equal of Mick O'Connell.

A few years ago I spend an unforgettable afternoon on Valentia Island at the invitation of Mick. Over the Portmagee Bridge which links the island to the mainland, and then the spectacular views from the various high vantage points as the heavy seas crashed against the rocks and gulls swooped and dived overhead. Mick took me on a sightseeing trip around the island, and it was very obvious that his heart was here.

Later in his beautiful home with spectacular views over the wild Atlantic, enjoying gorgeous freshly baked scones and piping hot tea served by his lovely Cavan-born wife Rosaleen, we discussed that year he led Kerry to the title. He first explained to me about the captaincy.

> The only reason I was captain was because South Kerry had won the county championship the previous year and I was the only person from Valentia, the local regional champions, on the team.
>
> We played Tipperary in the first round in Killarney and as we were kicking around before the game began Jerome O'Shea, also a South Kerry man, said to me, 'It's your turn to be captain today.' There was no big discussion about it, and anyway in my view the captain is not important in Gaelic games. The captain is just there to accept the trophy in Croke Park if the team wins. That's my view on it.

Kerry won easily that day against Tipperary and defeated Cork four weeks later in the Munster final in Killarney; the Valentia man had won his very first provincial medal and accepted the Munster Cup (a trophy, unbelievably, with no name) from the chairman, Jack Barrett from Kinsale. He would play in fifteen more Munster finals, winning another eleven medals. He recalled:

> Since our last meeting with Cork my game had evolved a lot, and the fact that I was captain was only incidental. Young Dave Geaney from Castleisland, making only his second senior appearance, scored 1–1 from corner-forward, causing a high amount of worry to Cork's Dan Murray. As a result of this win the Munster Cup for the very first time made its way to Valentia Island, my own little corner of the country.

Old rivals Dublin awaited in the semi-final. The whole country had high expectations, which were not disappointed. And Mick O'Connell had what many judges of the game described as his finest hour in the green and gold. It was a star-studded Dublin side, with household names who had helped the county to win the All-Ireland the previous year: Paddy Flaherty, Jim Crowley, Cathal O'Leary, Ollie Freeney, Des Ferguson, Paddy Haughey and the legendary Kevin Heffernan.

'Over 70,000 people attended that semi-final of 1959,' Mick reminded me, 'and more that a few who have seen a bit of football rate that as the most spectacular game of all.' The Island man was at his greatest that day. Fifteen minutes into the second half Kerry were eight points ahead, but within the space of six minutes Dublin got two goals and a point to close the gap. Kerry were now in big trouble, but O'Connell rose to the occasion as he won ball after ball both in defence and at midfield. The captain led his men to a 1–10 to 2–5 victory over their old adversaries. The All-Ireland final against Galway now awaited.

After an outstanding year in the green and gold, the final did not turn out as O'Connell would have wished:

> In my eagerness to make sure I would not fail through lack of fitness I trained harder than ever but, to my cost, not too wisely. Due to a combination of errors, not the least of which was the changing from my regular schedule of training, I had only done only harm to myself.
>
> In the very first quarter of the match I twisted my knee when contesting a high ball with Frank Evers and was in no condition to continue. However, the selectors must have thought my presence was of some psychological benefit to the team and would not allow me come off the field. They moved me to one of the forward positions but I was of no help to my teammates and after a short time I limped off to the dug-out.

While bitterly disappointed by his injury, Mick was naturally delighted for his teammates. 'I was just unlucky that day I suppose and it took some of the personal satisfaction out of it, but it was great to see Kerry win another All-Ireland and my friends win their medals. It was the first final I was involved in.' Kerry had won easily, 3–7 to 1–4, the goals coming from Dan McAuliffe (2) and substitute Garry McMahon. But it was Dr Sean Murphy who stole the limelight, giving a memorable display at right half-back. To this day when that match is spoken about it, it is referred to as 'the Sean Murphy final'.

As is the tradition, the captain was presented with the cup in the Hogan Stand after the game. Mick told me:

> In the usual way the Sam Maguire Cup was presented to me as captain but it remained in my possession for only a few minutes. Speeches over and amid cheers and applause, we began to make our way across the field to the dressing rooms. I was being shouldered high, aching knee and all, and very quickly the cup and I parted company. Where it went I had no idea.

While the rest of the Kerry team celebrated victory long into the night, Mick, never in the habit of attending receptions, caught the train home. Indeed, I have vivid memories of rushing for that train with friends and seeing Mick being mobbed by Kerry supporters as he boarded with some friends.

> Celebrations I can assure you were not on my mind that night, but the problem of securing my punt above the high-water mark when I reached the island that night. With a low tide and my injured leg

> I would have my work cut out for me. I was working with the cable company and all the others were going to work, so why should I get excused because of my sport? I was always back in my job the following morning after all matches.
>
> Dressing rooms were always filled with people anxious to handle cups and this was not important to me. Indeed after that 1959 win the Sam Maguire was somewhere in Waterville under a stack of tyres for a while. There was no hawking of the cup around back then. It was celebration enough for me to play and then come home.

Mick was reunited with the Sam Maguire a few nights later as it visited Valentia Island for the first time. He smiles as he recalls the occasion.

> I was lying in bed resting my injured knee when I heard the unusual sound of a band approaching and I soon discovered it was a parade of players and supporters and our trainer Dr Eamonn O'Sullivan bearing the trophy. It was the first time for many crossing water and a late ferry was laid on by Paddy Murphy to accommodate the travellers. Speeches were made from the back of a lorry and later the descriptions given were comparable to Chichester's account of the rounding of the Cape. It all added to my memories of captaining Kerry to their nineteenth All-Ireland title.

Winning cups and medals with club or county was never the ultimate goal during Mick O'Connell's glorious career. He once told me:

> Playing the game gave me the greatest thrill of all; it is a challenge

against oneself. Any time I got a ball coming from a distance was that challenge, the challenge to catch it inch perfect. I don't mean just beating the opposing player, that's incidental to the whole thing, but the fact that you judged the ball with perfection, leaped up and grasped it in full flight. That's the personal satisfaction that stands out in my memory of playing for club and county.

Wherever you travel in the world, when the name Mick O'Connell is mentioned, GAA fans young and old will immediately sit up and launch into discussions of his life and times, because Mick is, without fear of contradiction, one of Irish sport's true living legends. To meet him and spend time in his company is a very special privilege.

Mick and Rosaleen have two sons and one daughter. Now in his eightieth year, Mick remains synonymous with all that is great and good in Gaelic football: elegance, grace, skill, poetic rhythm, high fielding and long, accurate kicking. He was the most admired and graceful midfielder the game has ever seen.

The Kerry poet Brendan Kennelly wrote the following lines about O'Connell.

He had to reach the island in the winter gale
He pushed the little boat
Over the rough stones till she came afloat:
You'd swear he could see nothing when he hoisted sail
And cut the dark. Once, a grey shape blurred
Above his head while pitch black water slapped
And tried to climb over the side but dropped
Into the sea, thwarted. In time he heard
The special thunder of the island shore,

He hauled the boat in, sheltered near a rock
And smiled to hear the sea's defeated roar;
Breathing as though the air were infinitely sweet,
He watched the mainland where the hard wind struck.
The island clay felt good beneath his feet,
A man undeceived by victory or defeat.

Sean Óg Sheehy (1962)

When Sean Óg Sheehy climbed the steps of the old Hogan Stand in 1962 to accept the Sam Maguire Cup, he was walking into history. Sean Óg was emulating his legendary father John Joe, who had captained Kerry to All-Ireland victory on two occasions, 1926 and 1930. It was a momentous day for the Sheehy family, as Sean Óg's two brothers, Niall and Paudie, were also on the starting fifteen. A fourth brother, Brian, who had also played with the seniors, won an All-Ireland junior medal the following year.

Such a football pedigree could only belong to the purebred class. John Joe Sheehy had played a major part in Kerry's great success on the field. He won four All-Ireland medals, the last as Kerry captain in 1930, and he shocked the county that year when he retired from the game. He died in 1980 at the age of eighty-three when he was still President of the Kerry county board. The Sheehys and the Tralee John Mitchels club are synonymous. That's where the brothers studied and perfected the craft, and they soon graduated up the line – full recognition came when the trio lined out at Croke Park.

I have vivid memories of being a Kerry minor footballer in 1959 when John Joe was a selector. We had togged out for the Munster final against Cork in St Finan's Psychiatric Hospital, which overlooks Fitzgerald Stadium, Killarney, and made our way to the playing field through the crowds on the terrace.

Before the game commenced we gathered around John Joe at the halfway line, where he proceeded to deliver a rousing pep talk reminding us in no uncertain terms of our history, what we stood for, what the green and gold jerseys represented; he even recalled names of legendary Kerry footballers who had passed on to their eternal reward.

Sean Óg assumed the mantle of Kerry captain in 1962 due to the fact that his club had won the Kerry county championship the previous year – a hat-trick of wins. In fact, powered by the four Sheehy brothers, they would go on to complete a record five Kerry county championships in a row, which stands to this day and is unlikely ever to be equalled. Brothers Niall (1964) and Paudie (1953) also captained Kerry in the championship.

Sean Óg began that 1962 campaign at right half-back, and Waterford were defeated in the first round after a hard struggle, 2–18 to 2–6. For the Munster final against Cork he was selected at wing-forward as Donie O'Sullivan came into the defence. A disappointing hour's football saw Cork slump to a 4–8 to 0–4 defeat. The goals came from Gene O'Driscoll, Tom Long, Dan McAuliffe and midfielder Mick O'Connell. It was Kerry's fifth Munster crown in a row.

The captain returned to his more customary position at half-back for the glamour clash against Dublin in the semi-final, and led his men to a 2–12 to 0–10 victory over the Dubs. Tom Long with 1–3 and Garry McMahon, 1–1, sent the Kingdom on their winning way. Sean Óg was lavish in his praise for Mick O'Connell that day. 'He was brilliant, it was his day. His fielding was magnificent and his kicking with both feet has not been surpassed. He is undoubtedly the greatest exponent of Gaelic football I have seen.'

Roscommon now stood between the Tralee man and history, and in one of the most disappointing finals I have ever seen, Kerry easily overcame their opponents, 1–12 to 1–6. In an interview years later Sean Óg made no secret of the fact that it was a very poor game. 'Meeting my father afterwards was very special and he was delighted we won but I found it difficult to be too excited because the game was so bad. Terrible is the only word to describe it.'

It was the first final ever televised live, and a record was set that day which still exists, as I described in a previous chapter. The late Garry McMahon described it to me:

> Before the game Jim Brosnan told me that the Roscommon corner-back had a habit of attacking every ball that came in to the square. And sure enough just after the start Mick O'Connell floated a lovely free from the Cusack Stand side into the Canal goal; my man went for it full-blooded, missed it and I flicked it with my fist to the net. I had been a very good handballer in my youth, and I scored most of my goals for Kerry with my fist.

It was the dream start for Kerry, and they never looked back. Mick O'Connell again was brilliant, kicking eight points from play and frees. He actually finished 1962 as Kerry's top scorer with 1–16 to his name: an amazing achievement for a midfield player.

Sean Óg admits to having been very nervous coming out for that final, but recalled, 'Once I got a few kicks I settled down very well, but I get more enjoyment now in later life out of being captain than I did back then.' He had a relatively short career with Kerry, having had his first game in the league in 1961, and told me: 'I was dropped for the All-Ireland semi-final against Galway in 1963; Bernie O'Callaghan replaced me. I played my last game with the county against Mayo in 1964.'

For the 1962 final Kerry were forced to make one change from the Dublin game, for a reason that would be classed as laughable today. Donie O'Sullivan, who had played at corner-back in the Munster final and the All-Ireland semi-final, was a student in Maynooth College at the time. He told me: 'We had been allowed to play during the holidays, but we were not allowed out of the college to play. It was of course very disappointing as a young man, especially after helping the side reach the final. Noel Lucy came in instead of me.'

That 1962 win for Kerry came as a major surprise to many, as the county had been humiliated in the two previous years by a brilliant emerging Down side. The face of Gaelic football was changing dramatically.

Mickey Ned O'Sullivan (1975)

Croke Park, 28 September 1975, the All-Ireland final, Kerry v. Dublin. I watched the game from under the old Cusack Stand; a crowd of 66,346 was in attendance. We were pressed together like sardines: health & safety was not an issue back then. The late John Egan had given Kerry an early goal lead and then in the fifteenth minute an incident occurred that to this day is one of the most discussed happenings in an All-Ireland final. At the centre of the drama was the Kerry captain, Mickey Ned O'Sullivan. I had a clear view of what happened.

Kerry were attacking the Canal goal to my left, the rain was pouring down; Mickey Ned took a pass from Paudie Lynch and set off on a thrilling solo run into the heart of the towering Dublin defence. He skipped around two tackles and reached the fourteen yard line: it was a mission of sheer bravery but ultimately one of self-destruction. Two Dublin defenders, Alan Larkin and Sean Doherty, converged on the Kenmare captain, an elbow to the head stopped him in his tracks, and, as they say in Kerry, he went down like a sack of spuds and lay motionless on the ground.

Forty years later when I revisited the event with Mickey Ned, he had patchy memories of what happened. 'I soloed in as I often did, saw an opening and went for it, I remember getting a belt on the side of the head and then the lights went out. I couldn't breathe and thought I was going to die. My sight was gone, and I passed out and have no recollections after that.'

The medics rushed in; the game was held up for about ten minutes. The late John Moloney from Tipperary was the referee that day, but unfortunately he did not believe that the Kerry man was seriously injured, and even bent down and told him to get up. He did not warn any defender or even take a name. I became very friendly with John as I began my refereeing career later, and he told me that one of the biggest regrets in his great refereeing career was that 'I handled that situation with Mickey Ned very badly; it was a very dangerous foul and I often looked at it in video in the years that followed.'

The stretcher-bearers came on and the young captain was carried off the pitch and up the sideline, in front of where I was positioned. You could cut the tension with a knife. One of the Kerry selectors, Killarney chemist Donie Sheehan, was escorting the stretcher. As they walked past the packed stand Donie stopped, turned to the crowd and raised his two fists in the air in a gesture of sheer defiance. The Kerry supporters went berserk, roaring and shouting, and the chant, 'Kerry! Kerry! Kerry!' rent the air as the stretcher disappeared down the tunnel to the old dressing rooms. It was an amazing moment, and to this day I can still hear those sounds ringing in my ears. I have no doubt that the incident propelled the youngest Kerry team ever to go on and achieve a memorable victory.

Four hours later the captain woke up in the Richmond Hospital surrounded by nurses and doctors; he recalled that when they told him Kerry had won, 'I just felt empty.' He was discharged the following day and I remember distinctly meeting him in College Street, Killarney on the Monday night as the team was welcomed home by thousands of ecstatic supporters. It was evident that he had gone through a very rough time. He was pale, gaunt and not his usual exuberant self, and indeed many experts would say he never really came back to his very best form after this.

Mickey Ned had become the only Kerry captain in history to lead his men to the Sam Maguire but not receive it. His Kenmare district teammate Pat Spillane was informed by selector Denis McCarthy when the final whistle sounded that Pat would accept the cup. 'My acceptance speech,' Pat told me, 'was probably the shortest in history as I had nothing prepared. The head steward came to me and led me to the Hogan Stand and I had to ask him what the Irish was for "on behalf of". "Tá an-áthas orm an corn seo a glacadh ar son fhoireann Chiarraí." Probably the worst speech given by an All-Ireland winning captain.'

Thirty years later I was among over 700 people who attended a superb function and fundraiser organised by the Kenmare Shamrock GAA club in the INEC Killarney, when Mickey Ned finally lifted the Sam Maguire Cup in honour of Kerry's 1975 win. It was one of those very special occasions in which you could experience the real heart and soul of Kerry football. It was a magical evening.

Players from both the Kerry and Dublin teams of 1975 were in attendance, and it was the first time the two teams had been honoured collectively along with their managers, Kevin Heffernan and Mick O'Dwyer. It was an amazingly poignant moment for everyone present when Sean Doherty, the Dublin captain, presented Mickey Ned with the Sam Maguire.

Over €55,000 was raised for the Kenmare club from the banquet. The money went towards the funding of a new €750,000 sports complex which includes an indoor playing surface, changing rooms, a fully equipped gym, a meeting room and a kitchen. Also built was a 3,200 square metre all-weather training surface.

The Lord worked in strange ways for the Kenmare club when their exemplary captain was stretchered off Croke Park in 1975. Mickey's Ned's misfortune in a strange way helped his club secure the superb complex they boast of today in the Fr Breen Memorial Park, Kenmare. Was there ever a captain's story as inspiring as this?

Tim Kennelly (1979)

On Tuesday, 6 December 2005, the journalist Billy Keane, the son of the late great John B., was driving out to Beale strand for a clear-the-head stroll when he saw the ambulance outside Timmy Kennelly's house. 'He's gone, isn't he?' he asked a neighbour. And indeed the unstoppable, unblockable, unrockable Tim 'the Horse' Kennelly was gone, felled by a massive heart attack. No better man than Billy Keane to put memories of that tragic day into perspective, in an article published in the *Irish Independent* on 10 December.

> September 1978. The Horse was a giant sea rock between the Dublin storm and the Kerry goal. The water seemed to break up around him and spill away into waves as harmless as a puppy licking your toes. Kerry won. I ran onto the pitch. I was the second to get to him; Hanahoe was the first. Embrace. The happiness in his face.
>
> 'Tuesday, 4pm. 2005. There was a traffic jam building outside the house on the Ballylongford Road. The ambulance pulled out as Tim's son Noel arrived. It was sad to see a big, strong lad so utterly devastated. He was as polite as ever. Hugged and kissed before he went in

to see his father. His sister Joanne, a lovely gentle girl, found her Dad. Noel was very nice to her; he has the gentle way of his mother.

Tadhg the second son was in Australia where he was starring for the Sydney Swans. He would have to be told before the papers got to him. It had to be Noel. The two boys are very close and Noel said he couldn't do it. But he was bred to be brave, on and off the field. Noel woke his brother in what was the middle of the night in Australia. Tadhg immediately set out to see his Dad.

September 2000. Noel is the first of the Golden Age offspring to win a senior All-Ireland. Tim is in tears. There is no greater honour for a Kerry father. P. Ó Sé hops a ball. 'Timmy, you're throwing great pups.' I phoned Páidí just after Noel came home. Timmy and P. Ó just loved each other's company. They told each other outrageous yarns and pretended to believe them. Jimmy Deenihan was next to be told.

1987. The count centre in the Ashe Memorial Hall in Tralee. Deenihan heads the poll and is elected to the Dáil for the first time. The Horse wore out several pairs of shoes canvassing for his old teammate. Deenihan is carried shoulder high but the man underneath him is buckling. The Horse takes over.

'I've been carrying you all my life, Greek,' he says to Deenihan. Deenihan looks down and says 'That's what horses are for.'

Listowel was sombre and silent as the cortège moved from St Mary's church to the John Paul II graveyard. The funeral bell tolled mournfully. Thousands had paid their respects, including GAA personalities from all over Ireland. Kerry football heroes are afforded a royal and fitting send-off. It's special and unforgettable. Part of the heart and soul of Kerry football. Tim's coffin was shouldered through the town he loved so much by a relay of men and women. Massive crowds lined the streets. I was afforded the honour of being on one of those relay teams. The Kerry and Listowel Emmets jerseys lay on the coffin and a guard of honour formed by present and past players flanked the cortège. Stephen Stack and Jimmy Deenihan gave beautiful graveside orations, and a man who exemplified the traditions of Kerry with his displays of skill, courage, passion and bravery – a legend of the Kingdom – was laid to rest.

Tim Kennelly had been the inspirational captain for Kerry in their 1979 win over Dublin. The honour had been bestowed on him because the Feale Rangers divisional side from North Kerry had won the previous year's county championship, defeating Mid Kerry in the final. His teammates that day included Jimmy Deenihan, Patsy 'Skin' O'Connell, Johnny Mulvihill, Sean Walsh (who later became an outstanding chairman with Kerry and Munster), Tommy Bridgeman and the Bunyan brothers, Robert and John.

However, the manner in which Tim was appointed captain could only happen in Kerry, as I have seen down through the decades. There is always a bit of drama in relation to Kerry captains, as I have already mentioned. So when Feale Rangers had finished celebrating their 1978 Kerry win, the decision as to who would take the honour of leading Kerry had to be made.

In one of our many meetings, Tim explained what occurred. 'It was suggested that Jimmy Deenihan and I would toss a coin for the honour. We had a meeting on Good Friday and I was the lucky one to win. Jimmy as always was very gracious, wished me all the best for the year and I promised we would win the championship in Kerry again for him.'

And win it again they did, in 1980, beating the great Austin Stacks in the county final: the Tralee Rockies, with legends such as Dinny Long, Mikey Sheehy, Ger O'Keeffe, Ger Power, John O'Keeffe and Paddy 'Whacker'

Moriarty in their ranks. I have vivid memories of that dramatic game: just one of six senior county finals I refereed. Tim was playing centre-back and was magnificent, repelling attack after attack. However, ten minutes before half-time he went down injured. When 'the Horse' went down you knew something serious was wrong.

Sideline mentors and first aid came rushing to him; I stopped play and went over to ask if he was OK. 'I think I have broken my collarbone, Weeshie', he replied. He went off, then came back; he told me he was given a painkilling injection, and continued playing for the remainder of the hour. The arm was kept stationery and immobile across his mighty chest. It was a remarkable, brave performance, and he later revealed that Jimmy Deenihan had said to him, 'If you go off, Horse, we will be beaten.' Tim said, 'I played on. We won; Jimmy became Kerry captain, and led Kerry to four-in-a-row All-Ireland wins in 1981. I had kept my promise to my great friend.'

Tim Kennelly played all his games at centre-back that momentous year of '79, and the campaign began in devastating fashion across the Shannon in Milltown Malbay on 1 July when Kerry literally destroyed Clare on the massive score of 9–21 to 1–9. Pat Spillane, Ger Power and Eoin Liston with 7–6 between them led the way. It became known as 'the Milltown massacre'.

I put it to Tim in an interview that it had been totally unnecessary to destroy Clare like that, and they should have eased up on the scoring. He had his answer. 'There was fierce competition for places on the team, and there were many fellows on the sideline as good as you, waiting to take your place. You were on the team and Mick O'Dwyer was watching you, so everyone was watching their own corner.' Amazingly, Clare's 1–9 was the highest score against Kerry that year of Tim's captaincy.

It was a sign of things to come for Tim's team, as they crushed Cork in the Munster final 2–14 to 2–4. Tim liked to remind people that Cork were awarded two penalties that day but managed to score only one point from them. In the All-Ireland semi-final Kerry ran riot against hapless Monaghan, winning on a score of 5–14 to 0–7. It had been the Northerners' first Ulster Championship since 1930. They were completely overawed by the occasion in the semi-final.

Once again Dublin would be the opponents in the final; it was their sixth successive year in the decider. Mick O'Dwyer, Kerry's charismatic trainer, told me years later: 'In 1979 we were at our peak. We had some of the best players in the game and we had cover for every position. And Tim was an inspirational captain. Even when we lost key men before big games we were able to keep on winning.' In fact Ger Power missed the '79 final with an old hamstring injury and Tommy Doyle replaced him in attack.

The final was watched by a crowd of 72,185 and resulted in a comprehensive victory for Tim Kennelly's men: Kerry 3–13, Dublin 1–8. Tim was as usual a stone wall at centre-back and Kerry were supreme in all areas of the field. Mikey Sheehy, one of the greatest forwards ever to play the game, was at his brilliant best, scoring 2–6. Tim always maintained that Dublin brought out the best in Kerry. 'We were both trying to outmatch each other so it became a battle of two counties and all the rest fell further behind us. It was special when the Dublin players would come to the Listowel races after the final, and we all became firm lifelong friends despite the on-field rivalries.'

In one of the many interviews I conducted with Tim over the years, he revealed that being captain was a lot of pressure for him. 'I had a habit of withdrawing into myself before big games; Nuala understood this and she steered well clear of me and left me to myself. I would always study the man I was going to be marking and would learn as much as I could about him.'

Tim came from just outside Listowel: a lovely townland called Coolaclarig. He recalled when I interviewed him on my Radio Kerry programme *Terrace Talk*:

> My father was stone mad on football and brought me to all the matches. My first final was in 1962 when Kerry beat Roscommon, and it was very special for us because a Listowel man, Garry McMahon, was on the team and scored a goal after just thirty-two seconds. I brought the football everywhere with me, and when I went to bring the cows home in the evening I would solo the ball on the road behind the herd. I was football crazy and my father had a hard time with me as I was always ducking off to play football.

There was one incident he remembered clearly in relation to the final when he was captain; this probably captures again the heart and soul of Kerry, which manifests itself in so many strange ways.

> On the day before we left Listowel for the final I went to Coolaclarig to visit my grandmother, Hanna. She was a great woman for old customs and when I said goodbye and was going out the door she threw a shoe at my legs for good luck. And sure it worked, as we won the next day.

The longstanding tradition in Kerry is that the captain brings the cup to his home place on the Tuesday following the final. 'It was a dream come true for me to bring the Sam Maguire to Listowel,' Tim recalled, 'and there must have been nearly 25,000 people waiting. I'll never forget it.'

Tim and his lovely wife Nuala met at a carnival in Finuge, as she told me:

> He was just playing with the club at the time but later when he got on the Kerry team he would head off every evening to training with Jimmy Deenihan. His life was consumed by football and he loved it. We got married in 1978 just after the All-Ireland final; that was the year of Mikey Sheehy's famous goal against Paddy Cullen. But the big one for him was 1979, being captain, and to bring the cup home to Listowel was very special.

Tim's son Noel recalled himself and Tadhg having the 'hop ball' (banter) with their dad when watching videos of his career, telling him:

> He was lucky as he had a great team around him. He had fierce strength, and this I believe came from the farming. To be a winning captain of a Kerry team is a very unique thing. First you must win your county championship, and then get on the team, then win in Munster and then the All-Ireland final. We are very proud of our dad.

Nuala spoke of Tim's sudden death:

> We got great support at the time from everyone and it was a great help. We had been in Australia to see Tadhg win his medal in 2005 and Tim was over the moon with that. He said to me it would be his last trip and sadly it was. Football was Tadhg's life and I believe his father was the big driving force in that.

Tim, Nuala and Noel had been in Melbourne on the last Saturday in September 2005 to watch the Sydney Swans, with Tadhg starring, win the grand final. It was naturally a proud moment for all of them. Tim said:

> What can we say? It's just a fairy tale. I've witnessed All-Ireland finals at home, having played in them, but this is just unreal. Tension? There was fierce tension. I have a bit of a heart condition, and I can tell you one thing: it [the heart] must be a very, very good one to get through that and still be ticking. It was just beautiful, it's a dream come true for us.
>
> We're delighted and very proud of Tadhg. He's a very level-headed one. He came over here six years ago and we thought at the time he was facing a mighty test. His mum didn't want to let him go, but after a while we had to give in to him.
>
> He has worked so hard, the coaches have told me. He'd be there an hour before training and stay on an hour after it just to pick up things that he had to learn. I'm very proud of him.

In 2009 Tadhg returned to Kerry and helped them win the All-Ireland, thus becoming the only person to win AFL Premiership and Senior All-Ireland medals.

Following the momentous year of 1979, Tim continued playing for Kerry into 1983, having donned the green and gold since 1975. He retired following defeat by Cork in the Munster final. He was in an unusual position that year, as he was also a team selector, as he was in 1990. He was just fifty-one years old when he died: far too young.

John Egan (1982)

John Egan died suddenly at his home in Cork on 8 April 2012, aged just fifty-nine years. The retired Garda was one of my all-time favourite Kerry captains, but sadly he failed in the most dramatic circumstances of all to lift the Sam Maguire Cup on the steps of the Hogan Stand. John was captain of Kerry when they were denied a historic five-in-a-row All-Irelands by that late Seamus Darby goal in 1982. South Kerry had won the county championship in 1981 when they defeated Austin Stacks in the final, but before John took over the captaincy there was high drama around the appointment.

The year before John died I rang him at his home in Bishopstown in Cork, requesting an interview and saying I would travel there to meet him. Always the gentleman, he replied, 'No need, Weeshie; I will travel to Macroom and we will meet in the Castle Hotel.' Our interview centred, as expected, on the 1982 final.

He recalled the events surrounding the appointment of a captain as the campaign began that year.

> Ger Lynch was captain for the first two games; his club Valentia had won the South Kerry championship the previous year. However, not wanting the additional pressure of being captain, Lynch opted out and concentrated on holding his place on the team. St Mary's [Caherciveen] wanted Jack O'Shea to take over and my own club, Sneem, nominated me. So someone suggested it would be decided by drawing the name from a hat.

John's name came out first, and his destiny was decided. The young man from the little townland of Tahilla was Kerry's chosen leader as they set out to create history.

They played Clare first, then Cork (in a replay) and Armagh were defeated en route to the All-Ireland final. I have vivid memories of that year, as the county was gripped in five-in-a-row fever. The Cork ballad group Galleon launched a record anticipating a Kerry win:

> And it's five-in-a-row, five-in-a-row
> It's hard to believe we got five-in-a-row
> They came from the south, from the north, east and west
> But to Micko's machine they are all second best.

It was probably the most infamous record failure of all time.

Around the town of Killarney in the run-up to the final, five-in-a-row shirts, scarves, rosettes and hats were on sale everywhere. Trainer Mick O'Dwyer did all he could to dampen the growing hysteria, but the players were mobbed each evening as they left training, and the press corps laid siege to Fitzgerald Stadium. John Egan was in big demand as captain. He had always struggled with his weight, and I recall one evening, as I walked to town, meeting him on his own. He told me he had never been in better shape and had trained harder than ever before, 'I am heading home,' he explained. 'I did not go for a meal with the lads as I am watching my weight.'

The day of the final was one of high wind and torrential rain. I had refereed the semi-final between Offaly and Galway that year, and was very impressed with the patient play of the Leinster men as they won 1–12 to 1–11. Their patience was to prove their winning hand in the final also. The images of the closing two minutes in the final were burned indelibly into John's mind, and when interviewing him I was struck by the fact that he could recall every moment in minute detail.

> We were well in control of the game as we entered the final ten minutes. They got a few points from frees and I would say two of them were very soft; they proved crucial and helped keep Offaly in with a chance. I was thinking about my speech after receiving the cup. I was watching Offaly attack as I stood in the corner in front of the Canal End, then the goal went in and everything changed. I was then forever the man who captained Kerry to lose the five-in-row.

John told me about the event he believed ultimately cost them the title. It had all happened three months previously, while training in Fitzgerald Stadium on 1 June.

> I went for a ball with Jimmy Deenihan; we collided, our legs became entangled and Jimmy stayed on the ground. His leg was shattered, his year was over and he never played for Kerry again. He was a great tight-marking corner-back and I firmly believe if he had been marking Darby in that final he would have prevented their winning goal.

John Egan's dream of lifting the Sam Maguire Cup was not to be; he believed it was fate that denied him. But real tragedy hit him hard that winter when his twin brother Jerry lost his life in a drowning accident, and in the next three years he would lose his father and his brother-in-law.

He battled on and won his sixth All-Ireland medal in 1984, but was bitterly disappointed when he was substituted in the final against old rivals Dublin. 'I should have retired after 1982,' he confided in me. 'It had spelled the end of my career. The difference between being a winning Kerry captain and a losing one is massive. Win and you are surrounded by politicians, dignitaries, plied with invitations all over the place; lose, and you are simply forgotten overnight.'

John Egan was one of the greatest forwards I have ever seen; he never once lifted his hand in anger or raised his voice. Strong as an ox, he was beautifully balanced, with amazing control of the ball as he cut through opposing defences. In a magnificent career from 1973 to 1984 the man from Tahilla scored 35 goals and 118 points for his county.

His last words to me as we said goodbye following our meeting in the Castle Hotel, Macroom summed up for me the sheer agony of being a losing Kerry captain in an All-Ireland final. 'It was a brilliant game for everyone apart from Kerry. It wasn't for us, Weeshie; it hurts even as we speak about it. We should never have lost that game.'

Darren O'Sullivan (2009)

'For the honour of the little village.' One of the most memorable moments in the life of the captain of an All-Ireland winning team in football or hurling is when he is presented with the Sam Maguire Cup or the Liam McCarthy Cup by the President of the association on the podium of the Hogan Stand. As he lifts that cup above his head, the sight of thousands of supporters spread out before him on the green sward of Croke Park, displaying his county colours as they roar in approval, is undoubtedly an unforgettable and magical experience. However, not far behind this great occasion is the moment he lifts the trophy before his own people in his own town or village. This usually happens – especially here in Kerry – on the Tuesday or Wednesday following the final.

And so it was in September 2009 that I made my way to the beautiful seaside town of Glenbeigh – the gateway to the South – to see one of my favourite players, Darren O'Sullivan, receive adulation from his own people following Kerry's stunning victory over Cork in the All-Ireland final. Darren is with the Glenbeigh/Glencar club and was afforded the tremendous honour of wearing the captain's armband following Mid Kerry's great win in the previous year's county championship. The village was black with people. Every available vantage point was taken long before the bonfires blazed and the cup was paraded.

When you cross the beautiful little stone bridge, coming from the Killarney direction, you are in the parish of Glenbeigh/Glencar. It has its own Garda sergeant and priest. Fr Anthony O'Sullivan, a native of Ballymaclligott, is himself an All-Ireland medal winner. Football permeates all facets of life in this Kingdom. In his time as chaplain in St Finan's Psychiatric Hospital, Killarney, the good padre had helped it win the prestigious Connolly Cup. Yes, indeed: even the mental hospital in the county is obsessed with football.

Darren's football homeland is renowned for producing some superbly talented footballers. One that immediately comes to mind is Pat Griffin, who had been the last man from the club to lead the Kingdom around Croke Park on All-Ireland final day. That was in 1968, when Down once again proved too good for the men in the green and gold.

Others who carried this proud little club's flag for many years with great distinction included Mick Breen, Teddy Bowler, Jimmy Healy, Kevin Griffin, Mike Sullivan, Michael O'Grady, Owen O'Riordan, Denis Guerin, and Neilly, Peadar and Derry O'Sullivan. The Courtneys, McGillicuddys, Breens and Hoares all helped keep the flag flying in good and bad times. It was from this tradition that Darren O'Sullivan came.

The thousands of supporters had been pouring in since early afternoon. They came from the mountain and the hills, from near and far, and the local club under Chairman Jimmy Healy had everything organised to a T. It gave the opportunity to all the people of the area and beyond – young and old, mothers with babes in their arms dressed in green and gold, people in their eighties – to savour the unique atmosphere and experience the feeling of what their county is all about.

One man I met outside Ashe's Bar told me:

> This is a very special night for us. The big clubs in the towns of Kerry don't take as much notice when it happens for them and are well capable and used to catering for the huge crowds that attend the captain's homecoming. It's massive exposure for us, and only for the system we have in this county we and many other small clubs might never have this tremendous occasion you see here this evening. I hope this system never changes in our county.

I have often heard passionate Kerrymen debate at length the pros and cons of captaincy. Should the status quo remain or should it change to a system where the manager or county board nominates the captain? There was a motion (heavily defeated) at county convention some years ago to change the system. I was in Kilkenny for a few days recently as Radio Kerry travelled in force to celebrate its nine nominations for the prestigious PPI Radio Awards. Kilkenny's now legendary hurling manager Brian Cody was doing a book signing that weekend. His 2009 autobiography *Cody* is an excellent read. On the captaincy issue he states the following, which I endorse.

> I have no problem whatsoever with maintaining a tradition where the county champions nominate the captain, it had served us well. It's up to other counties to run their affairs as they wish and I see no reason

why we should change. I benefited from it myself in 1982 when my club won the county championship the previous year. It's a massive honour for the county champions to be allowed nominate the captain. Clubs are the very bedrock of everything we do, it's right we should continue to enjoy that perk. As far as I'm concerned, if it ain't broken, don't fix it. The manager may not always get the man who, in different circumstances, would be his personal choice, but that has nothing to do with it.

Problems with the captaincy

The stories behind the captaincy from the earliest days of Kerry football weave a wonderfully rich and diverse tapestry, and it would require a publication of its own to capture the agony and the ecstasy experienced by the men who led their county to victory or were deprived of the honour when it seemed within their grasp.

Gus Cremin died in 2014; he was Kerry's oldest living All-Ireland medal holder at the time. All through his exemplary life as a farmer he had harboured a great hurt, as he often explained to me when I was fortunate enough to sit and talk with him. In 1946 Gus captained Kerry in the All-Ireland final drawn game against Roscommon (his divisional side, Shannon Rangers, had won the previous year's county championship). Gus was dropped for the replay and lost the captaincy to Paddy Kennedy; he was introduced as a late substitute and Kerry won the game. Gus kicked the vital point to win the match, but was devastated at having lost the captaincy.

The following morning he took the train home from Dublin on his own. When the Kerry team arrived back in the county with the cup, Gus was out in the fields on his farm. Dr Eamonn O'Sullivan was the trainer at the time.

Gus told me that 'Dr Eamonn never wanted men like me, a farmer, to lead the team; he was always for students and others in white-collar jobs. I am firmly convinced of that.'

There was another strange twist to the captain's story in 1946. Eddie Dowling, also a Shannon Rangers man, had captained Kerry right up to the All-Ireland final: 'I took home the Munster Cup to Ballydonoghue; it was a great night in the village.' In training for the final he broke his leg in Fitzgerald Stadium: 'I clashed with Teddy O'Connor and the bone came out through the skin, Weeshie. I went to the final in crutches. I was told of course I would get a medal after being centre-field all year and being captain. The medal never came. It's one of my greatest regrets in football.' Two captains, two farmers, both badly wronged in the same year. The agony associated with Kerry football.

Kerry regained the All-Ireland in 1997 after a lapse of eleven years; it was one of the county's longest losing stretches. Once again the captaincy caused hurt and dismay, this time to two brothers. Mike and Liam Hassett were outstanding players and when their club Laune Rangers won the county championship in 1996, the captaincy was handed to the brothers. Mike captained the team to a National League win, and when Clare were defeated in the Munster final, 1–13 to 0–11, Mike was presented with the cup. Injury prevented him from playing against Cavan in the semi-final; brother Liam took over to lead Kerry to a win and a place in the All-Ireland final.

Mike recovered from his injury, was going great in training and expected to regain his place for the final. However, on the Tuesday before the game he was called aside and told he would not be on the team. Liam would remain as captain. When the full-time whistle went and Kerry were winners, the two brothers hugged each other on the field among the ecstatic supporters. 'I wanted Mike to go up and receive the cup, but he refused point blank,' Liam told me years later. 'If he had been even brought on as a sub it would have meant a great deal to both of us, and I regret to this day that we did not go up those steps together: I should have insisted that Mike was with me. Ben and Jerry O'Connor lifted the Liam McCarthy Cup together when Cork won the All-Ireland in 2004; we should have done the same.'

But worse was to follow. Just twenty-one official medals were given out to the winners, and Mike was not included. If the selectors had brought him on in the final against Mayo for a few minutes, he would have qualified. It left a bitter taste in the mouth of these exemplary Laune Rangers men: they hurt badly. Both of them left the Kerry panel, but when Sean Walsh took over as county board chairman he persuaded them to rejoin the squad. Kerry won again in 2000 and Mike got that elusive medal, but once again the captaincy had been the cause of some bitter words.

My own club, Killarney Legion, has had the honour of providing the Kerry captain three times. Denny Lyne stands apart as the man who captained Kerry in the only All-Ireland final played outside Croke Park; that was the Polo Grounds New York, 1947. Kerry were defeated by Cavan, and to his dying day Denny maintained that the referee's disallowing of two Kerry goals robbed him of being a winning Kerry captain.

Johnny Culloty captained the Kingdom to its twenty-first title in 1969, and stands apart as the only Kerry captain to have won All-Ireland medals as a goalkeeper and outfield. The outfield victory was in 1955, when the 'unbeatable' Dublin team was put to the sword. The third man from my club to lead the team was Diarmuid O'Donoghue, who was to experience the heartbreak of losing the captaincy. Diarmuid, father of the present Kerry star James, captained Kerry against Tipperary in the first round of the Munster championship in Tralee in 1984, by virtue of the fact that he had led a Killarney combined team to county championship victory in 1983.

Diarmuid, unfortunately, was not selected for the Munster final in Killarney and was denied the opportunity of leading out his county in his own town. Gneeveguilla stalwart Ambrose O'Donovan was handed the captaincy by the Killarney football committee. He proved to be an inspirational leader and Kerry went on to win that year, the centenary of the founding of the GAA.

To captain one's county to All-Ireland glory is the ultimate honour for any Kerryman; however, as we have seen, it has proved on many occasions to be a poisoned chalice and has caused heartbreak and massive disappointment. Nevertheless, the names of the thirty-seven men who have led their county to the Promised Land are enshrined forever in history's pages.

10

KERRY WOMEN: BREAKING NEW GROUND

Annie O'Sullivan was born and reared in Brasby's Lane, High Street, Killarney. When she died in 1949 at the age of eighty-three, she was afforded a guard of honour by members of my club, Killarney Legion: the first Legion woman to be recognised in this way. She was also the first woman I heard of who was involved in our GAA club in a direct way. Annie was the person who washed, dried and mended the club jerseys through the thirties and early forties.

The lanes of Killarney gave the town some exemplary people, and it was in Brasby's Lane that Annie reared her four sons, Billy, Neilly, Michael and Mattie. All four became members of the Legion club and Michael, popularly known as Mysie, took on the role of club bagman: he was responsible for the one and only set of jerseys worn by the senior team. After all games, he would haul his old brown suitcase from wherever the team had played back to his home down the lane and then, when required, his mother would take over.

The old-style heavy woollen jerseys would not wash easily. Annie would boil a big black pot of water over the open fire, pour it into the old tin bath and, with great devotion, hand-wash the green and white jerseys on the old scrubbing board with bars of Lifebuoy soap. Then, to dry them, they would be hoisted on the washing line strung across the lane from one house to another. If the weather was bad, as Billy told me, before they went to bed the jerseys were spread all around their little kitchen: on the backs of chairs, on the kitchen table and on the stair rail, where they were left until morning.

Annie was a great woman with the needle and thread, and Billy had vivid memories of his mother sitting by the gas lamp as darkness descended, 'repairing torn jerseys, stitching on big black numbers and replacing buttons lost in the heat of battle. Shirt buttons were used for this, often cut from our own shirts. She was a passionate Legion woman and loved the club.' Every Friday evening, Annie and other women from the lane would boil a big pot of stew and soup, made from pig's heads and crubeens bought cheaply from the one local butcher on the High Street, Mixi Hurley, who would throw in a few bones which helped greatly in the brewing of the stew.

Sadly, as Billy recalled, Annie slowly lost her sight as a result of her long nights sewing and stitching for her club and making and repairing clothes for her neighbours. Before her death she had become completely blind and the boys would read for her during the long winter evenings. Annie O'Sullivan was a remarkable woman who, like many of her generation involved in the GAA in some way, was seen and not heard.

Bernie Reen

The apple never falls far from the tree, and it was inevitable that Bernie Reen would become deeply involved in the GAA affairs of Kerry. Little did she think, however, when she attended her first meeting of her club, Rathmore, that it was the beginning of a journey that would see her become the very first woman to serve as an officer of the Kerry county board.

Born into one of the staunchest and most traditional GAA families in Kerry, Bernie was reared on a diet of football and hurling. As she recalled, 'Whenever the family sat down for a meal, the discussion was always about football, and I simply loved it.' Her maternal grandfather, Paddy Healy from Headford, was a legendary figure of the game. He won All-Ireland medals with Kerry in 1913 and 1914 and played with Dr Crokes. Her late mother, Birdie, loved telling the family the stories of her father milking the cows in the morning, rushing out the door with his football boots, socks and togs, getting the train to Dublin at Headford, walking to Jones Road, helping the Kingdom to victory and arriving home in time to do the evening milking. At times the train would make an unscheduled stop near his house; Paddy would jump off and make his way home through the fields.

Bernie's most cherished possession is her grandfather's 1914 All-Ireland medal; she told me that somehow his two medals finished up in America, 'we got one back and it was given to me, it's now over one hundred years old and brought out only on very special occasions. My grandfather was also deeply involved in administration and was always organising meetings and promoting the game in Headford.' Her uncle Timmy Healy, her mother's brother, played junior and senior with Kerry and was also selector for a number of years with the county teams.

One of a family of seven, she was born and reared next door to Fitzgerald Stadium, the spiritual home of Kerry football. The small pitch there was their playground, and long summer evenings were spent playing camogie and football. Her father, Mort O'Shea, played with the renowned Dr Crokes club and he also played hurling with Killarney; he was a county board delegate for many years, while her uncles Paddy and Sean O'Shea were also excellent club players.

However, it was her late mother who inspired and motivated Bernie in many ways:

> She was an amazing woman and simply loved the GAA. She was deeply involved in all aspects of the Crokes club. With my dad she attended every match wherever it was played; she washed the club jerseys for years, repaired them and, when a new set was purchased, it was mam who stitched on the numbers. She made the flags for the field and nothing was too much for her. She was always going to meetings, organising, contacting, and her whole life revolved around her family and the GAA. When she died, Sean Kelly told me at her funeral that she had been the very first woman to attend an East Kerry board meeting in Killarney.

Bernie Reen's GAA background is the embodiment of all that is great and good in Kerry football. Her brothers Pat and Seanie won All-Ireland club medals with Dr Crokes in 1992 and both played inter-county hurling with Kerry. In 2007, Pat reached the pinnacle of football management when he guided Kerry to a magnificent All-Ireland final victory over Cork. And so it was inevitable that this young O'Shea woman would go on and achieve great things in one capacity or another in Kerry GAA circles.

When Bernie married Denis Reen, they settled down in Rathmore. She later became immersed in her three sons' sporting pursuits: the Community Games played a huge part in promoting her involvement. However, she is adamant that it was not easy for women to break into the male-dominated GAA circles.

> I was determined to steer the boys into sports and especially the GAA; it becomes a lifestyle that is great for them and gives them a great appreciation of fitness. All three play and are deeply involved. When the boys were young the organisation was mainly male-dominated; women were involved all right in Scór and behind the scenes, but, I found, not encouraged to become deeply involved and indeed would be often frowned upon: those were my impressions. The club structures were far different twenty years ago, whereas now all clubs have their own meeting rooms and club houses which make it easier for women to attend.

Bernie's first tentative steps towards leadership in the GAA began simply enough and by sheer accident. Persuaded by her friend Dermie Moynihan in Rathmore to attend the club's annual general meeting, she told me:

> The secretary at the time, Donal O'Leary, was retiring, and before I realised what was happening, I was roped in and found myself as club secretary. All the usual promises were directed at me: 'you'll get plenty help, we are all there for you', etc., but I found myself not only secretary of this big club but also county board and East Kerry board delegate as these positions went with the position but, of course, I was not told until afterwards. So I was really pitched in at the deep end.

This was the best thing that ever happened, she recalled, and she simply had to be hands-on in all facets of club activity.

> My club chairman Kieran O'Keeffe accompanied me for my initial outing and I never realised I was entering an all-male domain where no woman had gone before, to the best of my knowledge. I sat at the back of the hall in the Austin Stack Park, Tralee, mortified. Sean Kelly was county chairman at the time and made a big thing of me being there and welcomed me; God, I then realised I was the only woman present. Now all the men were very courteous to me, I must say, but I still got the feeling that I was stepping into a different world and it was a very daunting experience, one that I never forgot.

Her four years as secretary of her club was a massive learning experience for Bernie. Attending club meetings, county board meetings, fundraising, notifying players re games, keeping the minutes of meetings, and the hundred and one tasks that fall on the shoulders of a club secretary. As she recalls, 'Raising my family on top of all of this was an extra burden but my husband Denis was my rock, and only for his help and encouragement I certainly would not have been able to continue. But I really enjoyed it and I was conscious of breaking new ground for women in Kerry football.'

In 2000, now completely engrossed in GAA affairs, Bernie felt she had even more to offer and decided to run for the position of coaching and games officer to the Kerry county board: the first woman to do so. Liam Sayers, a highly experienced worker, was her opponent and was elected, but Bernie learned a lot from the experience. When the post became vacant again in 2002, she threw her hat in the ring and duly became the first woman to take a seat on the Kerry county board.

The Killarney-born woman made a huge impact during her term and recognised the fact that coaching young footballers and hurlers in the county was vital for the future of the games. 'When I was elected there were just three full-time coaches in Kerry,' she recalled, 'my brother Pat, Donal Daly and Maurice Leahy. I travelled the whole county, went to all the district boards, schools, and clubs asking for financial commitment and we were very successful and got a great response, while the Munster council also chipped in. I spent some sleepless nights as very few people had any great interest in developing coaching.'

With Bernie's drive, determination and foresight, five more full-time coaches were appointed in the county. She even got a call from Croke Park advising her not to go down that road: to only appoint part-time coaches. However, wise woman that she is, she went ahead and had the county board make permanent appointments. Now, of course, it is the norm all over the country to have full-time coaches and the clubs and schools are the big winners here.

She laughed when I asked how she was accepted by the GAA men of the county as she travelled far and wide in pursuit of improvement in games and coaching in Kerry. 'I was treated very well, I must say. However, at times, there were comments such as, "Aren't you a great little girl with a family and all to be so involved in this?" I found it at times very patronising and all I wanted was to be taken seriously and judged on my work.'

In 2007, following five years in which she worked tirelessly for her county, Bernie stepped down from her role as coaching and games officer as a five-year rule had come into force in the association. She took a two-year break and then, with renewed energy, this remarkable lady broke new ground and returned as Munster Council delegate for the county. 'While I enjoyed my role, it required a lot of travelling to meetings outside the county,' she reflected; 'I really did not have the passion for this and the one thing I have discovered is that you must have a real passion for what you are involved in.'

Bernie served for three years as Munster Council delegate and, when the new position of child welfare officer was created, the board decided that she was the ideal person to fill it. It was a whole new challenge, and many issues came to light as she was now the intermediary between parents, clubs and county board. 'I was dealing with parents of boys and girls, some of whom had no great concept of the GAA, but I enjoyed it immensely', she told me of this very important position she still holds today.

Bernie sees big challenges ahead for the GAA in Kerry: there is huge pressure on volunteers and, with some of the smaller clubs having to amalgamate in the rural areas, emigration has hit Kerry very hard. 'I don't feel we are getting enough guidance from Croke Park in these issues, and we are not putting enough resources into club structures', she informed me. She would love to see women involved in the Ard Chomhairle of the association: it's too male-dominated and women have so much to bring to the table. She would also love to see the ladies' football and camogie associations work together as they have, she feels, a lot to offer each other, and all clubs around the country would become even stronger.

Her greatest fear is for the clubs of Kerry:

> We have a two-tier system in the GAA: Croke Park with all its full-time officials and, here in Kerry for instance, in our county board we have just one, Peter Twiss our secretary. We will have to be more flexible in our rules in relation to letting players move from one club to another; the rural clubs are being decimated and we need massive restructuring in the association.

Bernie Reen is a woman simply bursting with great ideas; she is a tonic to chat with and I have no doubt that she would be more than capable of taking on the job of chairperson of the Kerry county board. But, I asked her, would she be interested in becoming chairperson?

> Well, Weeshie, I don't believe I am cut out for that position: I am more of a grafter than anything else and there are more capable women than me, such as Maureen O'Shea who was PRO for a number of years. However, I suppose if the call came I might answer that call. Who knows what lies before us?

Jerome Conway was county board chairman for a time and worked closely with Bernie. He was high in his praise of the Rathmore club woman.

> I found her so passionate about everything she took on, fierce enthusiastic; she has great energy and is full of new ideas. Bernie was always on top of what she was doing and was so forceful in her ideas and could argue her point better that any man. She was a pioneer in many ways and her presence at meetings made us all far better at what we were working at. She is doing marvellous work as children's officer, and has pushed this on in a massive way in Kerry and has been directly responsible for the placing of children's officers in every district in Kerry. We are fortunate to have women of her calibre in Kerry.

When asked if Bernie would be capable of taking on the role of chairperson in Kerry, Jerome answered, 'She is capable of taking on any job in the association if she puts her mind to it.' The ultimate compliment for a remarkable Kerry woman.

COURTESY OF THE COSTELLO FAMILY

The All-Ireland-winning Kerry team of 1913/14, pictured outside Dunboyne House, Co. Meath, with the house's owners, the McCarthys. In the centre-front is Kerry captain Dick Fitzgerald, after whom Fitzgerald Stadium was named.

The legendary four-in-a-row All-Ireland-winning team (1929–1932). The side was trained by one of Kerry's greatest sons, Jack McCarthy from Tralee, seen standing on the extreme right. Not only a player, a trainer and a referee, Jack was also a founder member of Kerins O'Rahillys; chairman and secretary of the Kerry county board; and Munster Council secretary for forty-six years until his death in 1977.

My team from the Presentation Monastery, Killarney, in 1954. We won the East Kerry National Schools League in the famed Fitzgerald Stadium. I'm in the front, far right.

Left: The Kerry senior football selectors of 1955, deep in concentration. All are now sadly deceased.

Below: I achieved my first Kerry football dream in 1959 when I played in goal for the minor team. I am at the front, first on the left.

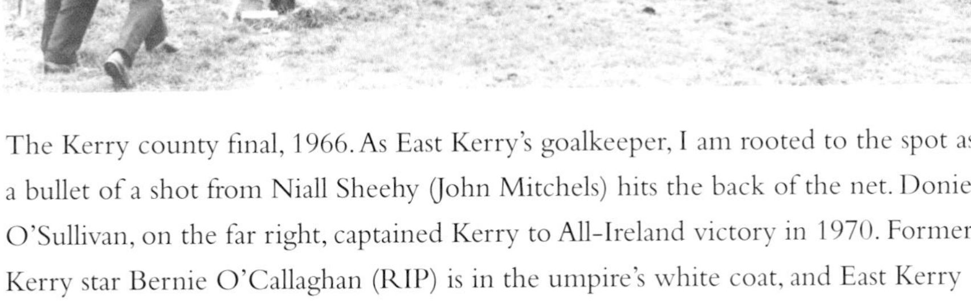

© PADRAIG KENNELLY, KERRY'S EYE

The Kerry county final, 1966. As East Kerry's goalkeeper, I am rooted to the spot as a bullet of a shot from Niall Sheehy (John Mitchels) hits the back of the net. Donie O'Sullivan, on the far right, captained Kerry to All-Ireland victory in 1970. Former Kerry star Bernie O'Callaghan (RIP) is in the umpire's white coat, and East Kerry selector Paul O'Sullivan (RIP) is on the far left.

© DONAL MACMONAGLE, KILLARNEY

I worked as a psychiatric nurse in St Finan's Hospital, Killarney, for thirty-eight years. When I first entered the service in 1962, there were over 1,000 patients and 500 staff within its high Victorian walls; today it lies empty. Football was a lifeline for patients and staff. Both fielded their own teams, and I often travelled to other hospitals around Munster and beyond to play matches. Here is the 1972 team, comprising nursing, kitchen and maintenance staff, who won many competitions including All-Irelands for Psychiatric Hospitals. I am in the front row, on the left.

At the other end of the lens: renowned Kerry photographer Julien Behal (right) with friends before the 2015 All-Ireland Final between Kerry and Dublin.

I have met Kerry supporters around the world, and this amazing Tralee man stands apart from all others. Elliott Keane is forty-two years old; he has a rare illness called dermatomyositis and is wheelchair-bound. He attended his first All-Ireland final in 1982 and still travels to every Kerry championship game. He exempifies the heart and soul of Kerry football.

The diaspora: Connie Kelly left Blennerville, outside Tralee, in 1965, landed in Boston, joined the Kerry GAA club there, and has served it in every capacity up to the present day. His wife Dolly and family (he's pictured here with one of his grandkids) are steeped in all that is great and good in the Kerry traditions.

Above left: Surrounded by Kerry legends. Front left: Mick O'Connell, Kerry captain for the All-Ireland win over Galway in 1959. Front right: Ned Fitzgerald, Kerry captain in the 1957 Championship and father of the great Maurice. Back left: Donie O'Sullivan, Kerry captain for the All-Ireland victory over Meath in 1970. And back right: photographer Christy Riordan, who has spent his life recording and documenting momentous South Kerry and Kerry football occasions and personalities.

Above right: James O'Donoghue is a star forward with my own club, Killarney Legion, as was his father Diarmuid. James is pictured here in 2014 with his GAA-GPA All-Stars Award and his Player of the Year Award.

In 1962, the Kerry Under-21 team won the first ever Munster title played in that grade, defeating Cork in the final in Kenmare 2–7 to 1–4. Fifty years later, the Munster Council invited the members of that historic side – myself included – to a function in Páirc Uí Rinn.

Kerry's women won their first All-Ireland final against Offaly in 1976, by 4–6 to 1–5. It was the beginning of a special time, and the organisation would go from strength to strength to reach the successful position it holds in Gaelic games today.

Above left: Maureen O'Shea was one of Kerry's greatest GAA workers, as an officer of the county board and in other vital organisational positions.

Above right: Mary Jo Curran won ten senior All-Ireland titles with Kerry and ten All-Star awards. Maurice Fitzgerald says he was influenced by Mary Jo's style of kicking – high praise from one of the best kickers the game has ever seen!

Above left: Brid McElligott-Rusk was chairperson of the famed John Mitchels club in Tralee and oversaw the development of its enormous new complex.

Above right: Killarney-born Bernie Reen, part of a famous Kerry footballing family, was the first woman to serve as an officer of the county board.

Kerry captain Geraldine O'Shea, one of the county's finest footballers, in action against Cork in the Ladies National Football League Division 1 Final in 2008. Geraldine also played international soccer for Ireland.

PHOTO BY SEAN KELLY

Myself and my wonderful family: (left to right) my son Kieran, my granddaughter Lucy (on her communion day), my daughters Denise and Carol Ann, my granddaughter Eva, my son-in-law Glenn Spellman and my wife Joan.

© EAMONN KEOGH, MACMONAGLE, KILLARNEY

At a civic reception for the Killarney-based presenters of Radio Kerry. From left: Sean Hurley, Sean Reilly, Mayor of Killarney Donal Grady, myself and Dermot Moriarty.

© SPORTSFILE

Uachtarán Chumann Lúthchleas Gael Aogán Ó Fearghail presents me with the GAA Hall of Fame award at the 2015 GAA McNamee Awards in Croke Park.

Brid McElligott-Rusk

When Brid McElligott-Rusk was elected chairperson of the famed John Mitchels club in Tralee in 2004, she became the first woman in Kerry to occupy such a position. She would go on to oversee the development of an enormous new complex as the Mitchels moved from their long-time home in Tralee town to an area just outside the town in Ballyseedy: a project that cost close to €11 million. I doubt that any other woman involved in the association in Kerry has left a legacy such as this; many men would shy away from the prospect of devoting ten years of their life on a voluntary basis to such a project.

The man who succeeded Brid as chairman of the club, Matt Moloney, is loud in his praise of her achievements, describing her as an amazing lady with wonderful leadership qualities.

> She is highly intelligent, greatly respected, gives 100% in everything she gets involved in and was always very approachable in all aspects of club affairs. There were times during the development that it appeared the whole thing was dead in the water but Brid kept driving it; she will be the first to tell you that she had a superb dedicated committee behind her. An amazing woman.

It was always going to be the Mitchels for Brid: from her very early days she has vivid memories of playing in the club field, attending matches and generally being immersed in the club's great traditions. Players such as the Sheehy brothers, Teddy Dowd, Joe Keohane and the O'Shea brothers were always the topic of conversation at home and among friends. As soon as she was old enough she became involved in various club committees as a natural progression: fundraising, organising social events, etc. 'Women back then,' she told me, 'generally kept in the background, and while we were involved in our club we kept a low profile. I always felt that it was our ability that was recognised, not our gender, and the club were very fair with us.'

Brid's abilities were easily spotted by the club members, and in 2004 she took over as chairperson, showing the way forward for the GAA women of Kerry. At this time the club had already tested the waters in relation to selling its old grounds of four-and-a-half acres in the heart of Tralee town. Brid explained the background to me.

> One of our biggest challenges was the fact that our catchment area in Tralee around the John Joe Sheehy Road had matured family-wise. You had very few families moving in and therefore we have very few juvenile players coming through. We faced a massive problem and moving was the only solution. The area was John Mitchels, but demographics heralded the dawn of reality: the place was old, out of touch, and we were falling behind our neighbours in the town.

The club agreed to sell the pitch for €10 million in February 2006: Brid chaired a special meeting on the sale which ended with 136 votes in favour and just one against. The die was cast, and Brid and her committee began proceedings. It was the beginning of a hectic period in her life. 'A deal with our first proposed tenant fell through but a new deal with Aldi supermarket group allowed the club to retain its club rooms, bar and restaurant in the heart of the town. It was a hectic time, and together with raising my family and continuous meetings I was constantly on the go.'

In 2014 the club made its historic move: only two miles, but a seismic shift to magnificent new surroundings just off the new Tralee bypass road. It will prove a win–win situation for the Mitchels, as Brid pointed out:

> The big thing is that we are debt-free since the move and there has been a lot of growth in the residential population on this side of the town, and our club would be the natural home for any youngsters who want to play football here. However, our traditional areas in Tralee town are still very important to us. Kevin Barry's Villas, Ballymullen, Marian Park and Boherbee will always be very close to our heart and history.

I have visited the new grounds at Ballyseedy many times and it is one of the finest complexes in the country. It includes four pitches, one all-weather and one floodlit; a 200-seater stand, a sports complex, twelve dressing rooms, a gym and sauna, medical and treatment rooms and a huge sports hall. Brid McElligott-Rusk has played a massive part in this transformation of this iconic Kerry club. Its county board delegate John Fitzgerald is in no doubt that she came along as chairperson at exactly the right time to drive the project to success. 'She was a great leader,' he enthused, 'and had phenomenal ability, passion and determination. When the relocation was in its infancy and when it stalled during the recession, Brid kept everyone going with her leadership.'

She would love to see more women put themselves forward for positions in the GAA.

> We have some amazing women in Kerry and of course it is difficult to combine raising a family with club work. It might be traditional with some people that women should be behind the scenes; however,

> if you have the drive and commitment you will succeed. I was always accepted and being a woman in the GAA did not cause any problems for me. Having a supportive husband is vital and I am extremely fortunate to have that person.

Brid believes that football in Kerry is part of who we are, and we should treasure it even more in today's world:

> It is part of our culture, vital to our communities, and all GAA clubs have a huge part to play in their localities. We must nurture the young talent and have a duty to the older citizens in our areas. We are very proud in the Mitchels to be able to say that this is part of our commitment. Last Christmas close to 200 of our older members attended a party in our club bar in the town: we retained this when we sold off the land to Aldi. We run bingo for our older people and have club masses; outings take as much interest in these people as in our young footballers. We are very fortunate to have very dedicated and committed mentors and managers who invest a massive amount of time in coaching and in courses which help to guide our young players. There is a great sense of community and family spirit in the club and we have seen a huge increase in our number of juveniles since we moved to our new facilities.

Kerry GAA has been blessed to have Brid. In my opinion she could very easily, if she so wished, become the first woman chairperson of the Kerry county board: she has all the attributes and her record is there for all to see. My last question to her was 'Will we ever see a woman President of the GAA?' Her answer was positive: 'It's not a matter of will we see it happen but when will it happen.' Indeed, I know a few women in Kerry who would fit that role perfectly.

Maureen O'Shea

Ventry (Ceann Trá) is a little village four miles west of Dingle town, with a post office, a pub, a shop and a Catholic church. The area is linked by the arc of Ventry harbour, with its magnificent sandy blue-flag beach which attracts visitors from far and near. Residents here are fluent Irish-language speakers and to hear them in conversation is a delightful experience. It is a stunningly beautiful area with glorious views of the wild Atlantic, and I have been told that on a perfect clear day you can see the coastline of America!

The area has given Kerry some of the county's greatest footballers. The late Páidí Ó Sé was born here, as were his famous nephews, Darragh, Thomas and Marc. Dan Cavanagh, who helped Kerry win the 1946 All-Ireland against Roscommon, also came from here, as did one of the finest I have ever seen – Tom Long, now resident in Killarney. However, during the forties and fifties especially, times were hard for people raising families in this area, employment was scant and emigration was common. It must have been very difficult for football-mad Denis O'Shea to pack his suitcase and head for New York in 1948, leaving behind family and friends and the opportunity of following the Kerry team, which he had done since he was a small boy.

On your way to Dingle from Killarney you pass through Keel, Castlemaine, a small village that also saw many of its people take the boat to America, especially during the fifties, when many of them settled in Hartford, Connecticut. And it was from Keel in 1951 that Philomena Prendergast followed those who had gone before her. Kerry football was part and parcel of her life also.

The Lord works in strange ways, and Denis and Philomena were fated to meet thousands of miles from their beloved Kerry, fall in love, marry and become proud parents of a beautiful baby girl. Just five months after she was born, Maureen O'Shea was on her way back to Kerry.

Maureen would to go on to become one of the county's greatest GAA workers, taking her place as an officer of the county board and acting in many vital positions as she showed the way forward for her fellow Kerry GAA women.

While Maureen will tell you that her great passion and love for Kerry football came mainly from her father, on her mother's side there is also a powerful connection with its history and traditions. The Foley brothers from Keel were cousins of her mother. After all these years, the phrase 'the Foleys from Keel' still resonates in the mind, reviving memories of a time long gone when the greats of Kerry football would be discussed on train journeys to and from the big games in Croke Park. Who was the greatest? Who was the best? Who was the most stylish of all? Who was the greatest Kerry footballer to emigrate? Always the same names recurred when the last of these questions was posed: the Foleys from Keel, Mickey Moynihan from Rathmore and the Hennessey brothers from Ballyduff, all sadly lost to the oceans of the world when emigration was at its peak in the hungry fifties. They headed for New York, the GAA was their lifeline there, and they became part of the greatest Gaelic football team ever seen outside these shores: the New York team, whose backbone, as you would expect, was Kerrymen. This team contested six National League finals, pitting itself against the best Ireland could produce; and there lining out against the league winners and champions of Ireland were the Foleys of Keel: Jim, Mick and Jack, powerful footballers.

The apple never falls far from the tree, and it was perhaps inevitable that the New York-born young woman would become involved in Kerry GAA affairs.

Ventry became her new home; Páidí Ó Sé was emerging as a Kerry legend and Maureen's father would take the family to every game Páidí played in. They travelled far and wide in support of their neighbour, and Maureen recalls Páidí handing All-Ireland tickets to her father every year that their county was involved. She believes that 'Without the influence of the Ó Sé family in Ventry it was very likely that I would not have been so obsessed with Kerry football.'

Maureen became a social welfare inspector and spent time in Cork and Limerick before returning to a permanent post in Kerry in 1990. She set up home in the parish of Ballymacelligott, a great sporting area situated about five miles east of Tralee with a long tradition of handball and GAA. World and Irish handball champions were born and bred in the parish: Sharon Daly, Sandy McSwiney, Maria Daly, Ashley Prendeville, Murty and Roundy McEllistrim and J.P. and Kelly Leen are some of the legendary names. Maureen took up the offer of becoming the handball club's secretary and later county board delegate.

Attending the male-dominated county board meetings proved no problem for this straight-talking Ventry woman. 'I had plenty neck', she remarked to me once. She is convinced that her involvement in union affairs in her day job gave her confidence. Her first few county board meetings were, she recalls, 'slightly daunting, but Bernie Reen was also attending at the same time and that was a huge advantage for me. Women were also beginning to have more freedom away from the home and the fact that I had a good job and my own car gave me the freedom to devote the necessary time to my new positions.' She learned the ropes as secretary and PRO of the Tralee Board, and praises Jimmy Foley, chairman at the time: 'We worked brilliantly together; he guided and directed me and was available to give the right advice.' Regarding the county board, she says:

> I found the work behind the scenes fascinating, how the committees and subcommittees were formed and worked, and I was put on the games and coaching group. Sean Walsh from Moyvane was county board chairman at the time and he always treated me with the greatest respect. As long as you did the work assigned to you were accepted wherever you went. I was also computer literate as a result of my work and this was also a great help to me.

While she never played the game, her interest in Kerry football increased, and when the position of PRO became vacant in 2008 she threw her hat into the ring. There was one other candidate, and following a tight race the clubs of Kerry elected their first woman PRO. 'John O'Leary of the East Kerry Board would have been the automatic choice for the position, but due to personal reasons he did not run,' she told me. 'If he had I would not have opposed him.' In fact John is now the exemplary PRO of the board. Looking back many years later, she believes that she did not prepare properly for the position.

> I should have become an officer of the board first, not PRO. There are four positions in my opinion which are the most vital and loaded with work: chairman, secretary, treasurer and PRO. I knew very few members of the board. Jerome Conway had become chairman; Eamon O'Sullivan was secretary: both were very helpful and encouraging but I found it very difficult at the beginning.

Maureen threw herself into her GAA work. She led the simplification of the system in relation to the hundreds of county fixtures. A company in Galway was approached, and within a few months all the Kerry fixtures were automated.

All secretaries in the county were schooled in information technology, emails became the accepted means of communicating, the postal letter became obsolete and Kerry GAA was dragged into the twenty-first century.

Her new responsibility also involved being hurling PRO for the county, and she freely admits that her knowledge of hurling and the Kerry hurling fraternity was poor.

> I resolved that I would devote as much time to hurling as football and I was not long learning the ropes and being fully accepted by the hurling men. I publicised the game in the county as much as possible both locally and nationally. I was responsible for all match programmes in the county and made full sure that all the hurling programmes were as good as the football. The people responsible for hurling in the county, both players and management, had a ferocious pride, passion and love for the game just like their football counterparts.

Regarding women and Kerry GAA, Maureen believes that 'It would not be a good thing to have more women than men on the county board. A woman's first responsibility is to her home and family. I did not become so deeply involved until my son was in his teens, and of course I have a great understanding husband.' Equality and the GAA came up a number of times in our conversation, and Maureen referred to 'Freedom to gain freedom: not a promise of freedom but a promise you can have if you want it. You can literally go anywhere in the GAA if you want to, even becoming chairperson of the county board or President of the organisation.'

Maureen believes that Bernie Reen and Brid McElligott-Rusk possess all the qualities needed to go on and become Kerry's first woman chairperson if they so wished. 'Why not? They have proved already in what they have achieved that they are well capable of going as far as they wish.' She would like to see the ladies' and men's organisations come together, and when she was PRO of the Ballymacelligott handball club she was deeply involved in the negotiations that united the women's and men's boards.

She sees no reason why a woman will not become President of the association in the years ahead. 'Tracy Kennedy has become the first female vice-chairperson of the Cork county board and there is no reason why she will not take the chair there in the near future, and of course Roisin Jordan made history in 2014 when she was elected chairperson of the Tyrone county board, the first female county chairperson in the history of the GAA.'

The new breed of Kerry GAA women have brought a whole new thinking to the organisation in Kerry. I expect that many more women will become active members of the county board.

11

THE LADY FOOTBALLERS

For years Kerry's women washed jerseys, made sandwiches and soup, served tea and cheered on the men, but until the 1970s it didn't occur to anyone that they too could be players. Could the great Kerry tradition, formed and nurtured in the men's game, be applied in the women's game too?

Ladies' football was played unofficially in Kerry in 1970–73, with clubs taking part in carnival tournaments etc. just for fun. Towards the end of 1973, in conjunction with a carnival week in Banteer, Co. Cork, Kerry and Cork were invited to play for a set of trophies. Mick Fitzgerald, who was involved with the Kerry camogie team at the time, and a Scotsman by the name of Alex Rintoul selected the Kerry team. It was the first ladies' football inter-county game in Munster, and attracted a large attendance. Cork football All-Star and All-Ireland medal holder Denny Long refereed, and Kerry won 5–10 to 4–11.

Even at that time there were some very talented players. Cork had a real star in Bridie Brosnan, who scored a goal and ten points, while Kerry's Mary Geaney contributed two goals and six points. Mary, from Castleisland, was an international hockey player and played a major part in these early days of ladies' football.

On 8 August 1974, a Kerry ladies' county board was formed at a meeting in the Austin Stacks GAA pavilion in Tralee. The board consisted of both women and men. The following officers were elected: chair, Richard Williams, Fossa Killarney; secretary, Joan Kelliher, Killarney; treasurer, Pat Lawlor, Ardfert; selectors, Mick Fitzgerald, Alex Rintoul, Richard Williams, Pat Lawlor.

A few club teams were formed around that time and a county league was held. The Munster Championship was played in a league system. Kerry played Cork in the first round and won with a few points to spare. They then played Waterford and won. Kerry played Tipperary in the Munster final at Kilsheelan, Co. Tipperary on 15 September. Tipperary won, 2–6 to 2–5, and went on to win the first All-Ireland ever played.

That historic first ever Kerry ladies' team: Sue Moloney, Josephine Dillon, Marion Quill, Eileen O'Shea, Mary O'Connor, Sheila Donnelly, Bernie Donoghue, Marie Murphy, Esther Murphy, Mai Lombard, Mary Geaney, Margaret Lawlor, Jenny Mason, Margaret Doherty, Helen Slattery.

Mick Fitzgerald, a retired Garda living in Castleisland, can be referred to as the father of Kerry ladies' football; he was there from the very beginning and helped set up the first county board. He comes from the village of Killimor in Galway and on his posting to Kerry got involved in coaching the Lixnaw hurlers and the Castleisland camogie side. Mick was present at the first meeting of the new ladies' board in Hayes's Hotel, Thurles in 1974. He was President of the association (1982–85) and has served as national treasurer for over twenty one years: truly one of the great GAA servants.

Mick was also a selector or manager in all of Kerry's All-Ireland triumphs at senior level, and was involved from start to finish in the great Kerry nine-in-a-row winning team. He was presented with the highest honour in the game, the President's Award, in 2008, and his comments to me were typical of the man:

> This came as a total shock to me but I accept it as a recognition for all that have been involved and have worked alongside me down through the years. I have loved every minute of my involvement in ladies' football and we had some marvellous memories. When we set the association up back in 1974 we never thought that the game would grow like it has. I am immensely proud of the association. Ladies' football is making tremendous strides and I am confident that the association and the game will go from strength to strength.

Fitzgerald was incorporated into the Ladies' Football Hall of Fame in 2004.

Kerry's women won their first All-Ireland final against Offaly at Littleton, Co. Tipperary on 10 October 1976, by 4–6 to 1–5. A handful of supporters travelled from Kerry for the fixture. Noreen Thompson at right full-back for Kerry gave a wonderful exhibition of fielding and must have broken the hearts of Offaly with her performance. Once more the leading scorer for Kerry was centre half-forward Mary Geaney, with 3–2. The other Kerry scorers were Nora Donoghue (1–1), Kathleen Brosnan (0–2) and Eileen Donoghue (0–1). That Kerry team: Sue Curtin, Noreen Thompson, Bernie Donoghue, Sue Moloney, Margaret Lawlor, Marie Murphy, Annette O'Connor, Dell McLoughlin, Nora Donoghue, Kathleen Brosnan, Mary Geaney (capt.), Mai Lombard, Eileen Donoghue, Margaret Doherty, Helen Slattery. Sub: Jackie Moriarty for Margaret Lawlor (injured). Other subs: Ann O'Connell, Amelia Collins, Mary Ferris, Eileen O'Connor, Matilda McDonagh.

The team and officials knew that when they arrived home there wouldn't be any bonfires, crowds or celebrations. The result of the game wasn't even in the national newspapers. Women put just as much work and preparation into their game as their male counterparts. They take as much pride in wearing their county jersey, no doubt at far greater cost to themselves; they should in my opinion be appreciated much more. The women's game has just as much excitement, just as many highs and lows, thrills and tense moments as the men's game; it's just that fewer people know about it!

As far as Kerry were concerned it was a great victory, and a wonderful feeling to win an All-Ireland. It was the beginning of a special time, and the organisation went from strength to strength to reach the very successful position it holds in Gaelic games today.

I asked Mick Fitzgerald who was the greatest footballer he had seen. He replied:

> Mary Jo Curran was head and shoulders above all others. She had no equals on the field of play. Tall, slim with great hands, one of the best fielders of the ball the game has seen. And remember back in her playing days all frees were taken from the ground and she had this skill mastered also. Her record speaks for itself.

Mary Jo Curran is unique in ladies' football as she has won ten senior All-Ireland titles with Kerry and ten All-Star awards. Her performances at centre-forward and midfield were a major factor in Kerry's golden age between 1982 and 1993. She was honoured with the 2013 Hall of Fame. Kerry's legendary forward Maurice Fitzgerald says that he was influenced by Mary Jo's style of kicking: 'We marvelled at her ability to kick with the left and right comfortably and to pull the ball down and send it over the bar from all angles.' High praise from a man recognised as one of the best kickers of a ball the game has seen.

Mary Jo is still involved in ladies' football with her club, Beaufort, and in 2015 was again part of the backroom team for the Kerry seniors. Her contribution to community life makes her stand out, although she tends to avoid the limelight if possible. I have interviewed her on a few occasions, and she once remarked:

> All I'll say is that I feel privileged to have been involved in sport. Any money spent in sport around the county and any investment in sporting facilities, you will get it back ten-fold because, as the children grow up, it's somewhere for them to go – not just physically but socially and mentally too, indeed in every area of their development.

When I am asked who were the greatest Kerry footballers, male and female, I have ever seen, my answer is 'Jack O'Shea and Mary Jo Curran'.

When Bridget Leen looks back at her football career, one year stands out. In 1984, Bridget had the honour of captaining what was probably the greatest women's Gaelic football team the game has seen (although the present Cork side will be also remembered among the greats). One of only a handful of footballers, male or female, to have won ten senior All-Ireland medals, Bridget – a native of Ballymacelligott who played with Castleisland – is now manager of O'Mahony's bookshop in Tralee, and recalled for me that special year in her sporting life.

> We had a brilliant team at that time, great players like Mary Jo Curran, Marian Doherty, Eileen Donoghue and Margaret Lawlor. We were

> going for three in a row All-Irelands and there was great pressure on the girls. We beat Limerick, Cork and Waterford to win the Munster championship. We travelled to Wexford for the All-Ireland semi-final and won by four points against the home county, and then in the final played in Timahoe, Co. Laois we were too good for Leitrim.

The homecoming was a dream come true for the Ballymac girl:

> I remember well going down Denny Street in Tralee on the back of a lorry standing alongside Ambrose O'Donovan, the captain of the Kerry seniors who had also won the All-Ireland. The place was black with people and there was I with the Brendan Martin Cup, and I remember thinking 'It's so tiny compared to the Sam Maguire held by Ambrose!'

As the years unfolded and the ladies won year after year, the Kerry public sat up and became very proud of the team. The local and national media began to give much more coverage to the game; Radio Kerry came on stream, as did the local papers, *The Kerryman* and *Kerry's Eye*. The cup was being shown around the county, visiting schools, clubs and social functions, and the players began to enjoy national prominence. More clubs were formed in the county and more young girls wanted to play the game with their schools and clubs, so the following for the ladies' game continued to grow; it occupies a very prominent position today.

That Kerry side went on to win six more All-Irelands and remained undefeated until 1991: a remarkable achievement. Bridget recalled:

> We trained like professionals and were probably ahead of our time. Mick Fitzgerald was an inspirational trainer and there was often weeks when I would go to the field five nights in a row. We raised our own finance, and often after a night's hard training we would set off raising money, selling lines or tickets, knocking at doors: we were a very united bunch of Kerry girls.

Things have changed greatly, according to Bridget, in the intervening years. In her time it was difficult even to be assured of having a field for training, and the women would sometimes have to move off the field if the men's teams wanted to play or train. 'Now of course,' she says, 'there are far more pitches dotted all around the county and clubs are very generous in accommodating the county ladies.' Watching Mick O'Dwyer's great side winning the All-Ireland fuelled Bridget's passion to play for Kerry in Croke Park.

She praises the coverage the ladies receive on television: to have TG4 televising most of the championship matches is a huge boost to the game. One disappointing factor she points out is the big drop-off in players when they reach a certain age, although there are far more girls playing the game in Kerry now than ever before.

Girls get married and have families; time will not permit them to train, travel and play; they leave the county seeking work; the game is not as organised as the men's game; some simply lose interest in the game. There are still not as many young girls playing as boys. The same applies to camogie in the county in relation to hurling. However, the ladies of today are have the very best facilities and the county board, under chairman Paddy White, leaves no stone unturned in supporting their efforts to win the coveted All-Ireland title.

Sarah Houlihan of Laune Rangers is one of the top players in the county at present and has been starring for Kerry for around eight years. She started playing in primary school, was trained by her dad and, as she told me, is 'completely obsessed by football'. A player with brilliant ball control and great speed, Sarah has won two Munster Championship medals and two All-Star awards, the top honour available; she has played in one All-Ireland final, losing to the all-conquering Cork team.

Her training regime is as gruelling as that of any of her male counterparts: on the field Wednesday, Friday and Sunday, and gym work two other days; little or no social life and strict dietary habits. 'Your life is on hold as the season progresses, and if you don't put in the work you will be found out very quickly', Sarah explained. 'Really we are very well looked after', she added, although travelling expenses for women are not adequate, in Sarah's view. The senior club championship in the county also needs to be improved, as 'Some girls are left without club football.' Pat Hartnett and Robbie Griffin, who have given years of dedicated service to the ladies' game in Kerry, agree on this point.

Sarah praised the publicity the ladies' game in the county receives from local press and radio, but feels that attendances are disappointing. She is living the Kerry dream, playing for her county, training all year around, playing in Croke Park, talking football and giving her all for her beloved green and gold. She is a credit to the game.

The last Sunday in September sees Croke Park play host to all three of the Ladies' Gaelic Championship finals (junior, intermediate and senior). With the Hill decorated and mini games of kids and mothers at all the half-times, the day is one of a kind. Attendance is steadily growing, and it is one of the best-attended female-only sports events in the world.

The Ladies' Gaelic Football Association (LGFA) has come a long way since 1974. It has over 150,000 members and seventeen full-time employees, ten of whom are based in Croke Park. With over 1000 clubs in Ireland and membership growing by the day, ladies' Gaelic is reaching women and girls from all over the country. There are also many overseas clubs, one of the latest additions coming from Cape Town in South Africa. In 2015 the Women's FA Cup final at Wembley Stadium recorded an attendance of 30,710; here a crowd of 31,083 attended the ladies' All-Ireland finals: an increase of over 3,000 on the previous year's figure.

LGFA President, Marie Hickey from Ballylinan, Co. Laois, says that:

> We are very ambitious for the future of our games; if we do not aim for progression then we will stagnate, and that is not what this sport is about. We have some of the best players in any sport playing our game and some that will be remembered in history as trailblazers and barrier-breakers.

In Kerry, close to 3000 players are registered with county secretary Mary Courtney and there are thirty-six clubs: a far cry from 1974, when Mick Fitzgerald and a few others saw a handful of players and two clubs begin an amazing journey for the women of Kerry.

12

MY ALL-TIME MOST SKILFUL/CLASSY/ STYLISH KERRY FIFTEEN

One often sees the term 'class' applied to players of various sports. But how is class defined in a Gaelic footballer? I decided to take the bull by the horns and pick the fifteen Kerry footballers whom I would consider the most stylish, classy, elegant and skilful of all. I am fully aware that many will disagree with my selection, and this is what makes it worthwhile in many ways.

I first contacted my great friend from Moyvane, Gabriel Fitzmaurice. Gabriel is the author of more than forty books, including many poetry collections, and has edited collections of essays including the works of the great John B. Keane. He is also a passionate follower of our national games, and I hope that some day he will take the time to publish his thoughts on them.

So, no better man to define the word 'class'. He responded with the following: 'A class player is one who deports himself with elegance and grace on the field of play and whose strength and beauty are an integral and effective part of his game.' Perfect, I thought. Now to attempt the near impossible and choose my fifteen: in doing so I confine myself to Kerry players I have seen from 1955 to the present day.

Goalkeeper: Johnny Culloty (Killarney Legion)

While you might imagine that the goalkeeper would be the most difficult choice of all, in fact it was clear-cut and I decided without hesitation to go for my own club man. Johnny was a brilliant forward in his young days, winning an All-Ireland medal at corner-forward with Kerry in 1955, and he brought all those outfield skills, class and style to his new position when he went between the sticks following a serious knee injury in 1956. His was an era when goalkeepers were fair game for the incoming forward, and Culloty would dance, dodge and weave his way out to clear as opponents attempted to bundle him, ball and all, into the back of the net. His skill as a hurling keeper for Kerry was also a joy to behold. He has a unique record of playing in goal for the Kerry minor hurlers at just fourteen years of age when he lined out against Limerick in the Gaelic Grounds, Limerick in 1952.

Johnny's All-Ireland winning career, spanning fifteen years from his first medal in 1955 to his last in 1970, must be some kind of a record. Is there a longer winning period for a Kerry footballer? One save that is forever spoken about was in the 1969 All-Ireland final against Offaly. It was the defining moment in the game. Just after half-time a long, high ball into the Kerry square at the Railway End of Croke Park was fielded by the Offaly full-forward Sean Evans, who turned and shot for goal in one movement. Culloty, in the perfect position, dived to his left, gathered the ball and cleared downfield. Kerry were just two points ahead. Micheál Ó Muircheartaigh, the renowned broadcaster, told me once that 'Offaly would definitely have won that All-Ireland only for that save. Johnny was a very calculating goalkeeper and he had a great sense of positioning, and with that forward instinct he had learned outfield he was a great man to clear the ball and put somebody in possession.'

That final saw Kerry win their twenty-first title, and Culloty was the captain. He became the first man from the town to bring the Sam Maguire to Beauty's Home. (The previous Killarney townie to captain a winning Kerry team in the final was the legendary Dick Fitzgerald in 1913 and 1914: the Sam Maguire Cup had not yet been presented to the association back then.)

I had a close and personal friendship with Johnny during his football career, in which he played in twelve Munster finals (winning ten) and nine All-Ireland finals (winning five). We both worked as psychiatric nurses in St Finan's Hospital, Killarney, and we both were inter-county goalkeepers but played outfield for our club, which was unusual. He was a fitness fanatic – ahead of his time, really – and during the long winter months after a day's work in the crowded hospital wards we would tog out and go running on the roads around the town. We lived in O'Sullivan's Place, and we would often run from there to Kilcummin Church and back, a distance of eight miles. We also trained in the dark on Killarney golf course, or scaled the gates at the Killarney racecourse and did five or six rounds of the track and a number of sprints. So when the summer training began we were always in very good physical condition.

Johnny was one of the most versatile and talented all-round sportsmen ever to come out of the Kingdom. He represented his county at football, hurling and basketball and was also a very talented golfer, oarsman, and snooker and billiards player. He is now of course long retired from St Finan's Hospital, with which he also won two All-Ireland medals as an outfield player. He continues to live in Killarney town and to work for his club. His wife Joan, two sons and two daughters are also deeply involved in the club.

Right full-back: Seamus Murphy (Camp) (RIP)

Rarely when you hear Kerry legends being discussed will you hear the name Seamus Murphy. Seamus was described to me by another former great Kerry player, John Dowling, as the most underrated player ever to grace a football field. The man from Camp in West Kerry starred for his county at midfield and in defence. He came out of retirement in the late sixties to win two medals at corner-back, 1969–70. I trained with him and played in goal behind him on a few occasions and had a close-up of his wonderful skills. Simply a class act, Seamus had a great pair of hands, he could read the game better than most and he was one of the best I have seen to shepherd an opponent to the corner flag and eventually block his attempt at a kick for goal. His skill in covering/marking was a wonderful art to watch at close quarters, and his man rarely scored off him.

Seamus seldom if ever fouled, and in my opinion would walk onto any of the modern teams. He won eleven senior Munster medals with Kerry – an amazing record – and never lost a game in the province. His wonderful skills and style were first appreciated when he attended school at Coláiste Íosagáin, Ballyvourney, Co. Cork (now closed); he won a Sigerson Cup with UCD and was a regular member of the Munster Railway Cup teams in the sixties. His brilliant career spanned three decades and he is the holder of four All-Ireland medals, having played in eight All-Ireland finals. Seamus played with Kerry from 1958 to 1971. Like many West Kerry footballers, his fielding ability was magnificent. In 1959 as Kerry beat Galway in the final, Seamus was midfield with the great Mick O'Connell. It was a special day for the Murphy family, as Seamus's brother Sean was man of the match.

Seamus set records in versatility that will never be equalled. In a span of twelve years or so he filled no fewer than ten positions on Kerry teams. In eight All-Ireland final appearances he played in five different positions. Nobody else in the history of the GAA can lay claim to such a record. Seamus had that lithe, sinewy build that is ideally suited to Gaelic football, being neither too big nor too small. He was an immaculate fielder; a brilliant reader of the game; his judgement was flawless; he could kick equally well with both feet; and his ability to block down an opponent's kick was an unforgettable feature of his play.

Seamus is also fondly remembered for his humility and friendliness, his devotion to his family and his helpful nature in the line of his work. He was Chief Agricultural Officer with Teagasc, taught at the Warrenstown agricultural college in Co. Meath, and worked as a presenter with Radio Kerry for a number of years. Seamus died in 2000 at just sixty-two years of age.

Full-back: John O'Keeffe (Austin Stacks)

John was affectionately known as 'the King', for very good reasons, and generally dominated his area of the field. Known to all as 'Johnno' he played in seven All-Ireland finals, winning five medals in the full-back position (just like Joe Keohane) to add to his previous two captured in 1969–70. He was a sub in the 1969 victory over Offaly, Kerry's twenty-first title, and centre-back the following year against Meath, the day Din Joe Crowley scored the goal of the century. John holds twelve Munster medals, six National Leagues, eight Railway Cups, four All-Stars, two All-Ireland clubs, four county championships, a Texaco Footballer of the Year and a Hogan Colleges Cup. He also partnered Mick O'Connell at midfield in a number of games. A hip injury which later in life necessitated a replacement brought his magnificent career to a premature end following the 1982 defeat to Offaly. Only for this he would probably have gone on to set a record for All-Ireland medal wins.

Johnno was quiet and modest, never one to brag, and simply oozed style and class in his every movement on the field. Six foot plus and built to match, he was a beautiful mover on the field. He displayed a wonderful sidestep and was an immaculate fielder; rarely did I see him commit a foul and be spoken to by a referee. Legendary sportswriter, Castleisland man Con Houlihan, wrote after the 1975 final win over Dublin: 'John O'Keeffe, of course was superb – but we would have been surprised at anything less of him. He is a model footballer blessed with wonderful skills and sporting as he is skilful.' John Barry, one of the doyens of *Kerryman* GAA reporters, said of his Austin Stacks clubmate following that match: 'Not once in the game did he put a foot wrong. It was another brilliant exhibition of full-back play by Johnno.' Is his All-Ireland medal-winning span from 1969 to 1981 a record for an outfield player?

Blood – especially Kerry blood – is thicker than water, and Johnno's father Frank played in the historic New York All-Ireland final of 1947. It was inevitable that once Johnno went to college in St Brendan's Killarney, the cradle of Kerry football, he would blossom. And so he did, leading the famed nursery as captain to a Hogan Cup win in 1969. He was just eighteen years of age at the time. I was part of the Kerry panel that year and Johnno was brought straight into Kerry training following the college victory, so I had a close-up view of this up-and-coming star. It was obvious that here was a very special young man.

Johnno is now retired from his job as teacher in Tralee CBS, whose teams he trained for many years. He is living in Tralee and keeps the body in top shape as he cycles the roads of Kerry winter and summer. He also writes a very informative GAA column for the *Irish Times* and has been coach to Limerick and Clare as well as physical trainer to Kerry under manager Páidí Ó Sé. He worked with the Kerry hurlers alongside his clubmate and friend Ger Power, and he had the honour of coaching the Irish International Rules team with Offaly great Matt Connor as selector in 2003 and 2004. With the UCD team, he won a Dublin County Championship in 1974 and the Leinster Club Championships and All-Ireland Club Championships in 1973–74 and 1974–75. He also won Sigerson Cup medals in 1973, 1974 and 1975.

John O'Keeffe is one of the all-time great players – his record proves that. For me, so fortunate to have seen him all through his career, his magnificent skill, sheer class and sportsmanship are memories I cherish when his name comes up for debate. One of the nicest gentlemen I have ever met.

Left full-back: Paudie Lynch

There were a number of contenders, but I finally decided on the great Beaufort man. This most elegant of players had wonderful hands and would simply glide past opponents. He had a beautiful sidestep and his fielding ability was exceptional; he was Mr Versatility, a trait that only the greatest and most skilful possess. Mick O'Dwyer told me: 'He could play in so many different positions it probably came against him in a way. He performed superbly in every position he played, and that's the real test of a great player. If he played in one position all his life he'd be regarded as one of the greatest players of all time. He would be on any great team of any period.' The ultimate tribute from the Kerry legend.

Standing over six feet tall, with great natural strength, for me Paudie is one of the most underrated Kerry footballers. He began his career at midfield with

Mick O'Connell in 1971. The bigger the occasion, the better he was. He lined out for his county in National League finals at midfield, right half-forward; centre-back and full-back and in All-Irelands at midfield, wing-forward and centre-back; in the 1980–81 All-Ireland wins he starred at corner-back. He won five senior medals and his older brother Brendan won three; uniquely, Brendan's final wins were at different playing times: sixty, sixty-five and seventy minutes.

After national school Paudie attended St Brendan's Seminary in Killarney, and it was here in 1969 under the captaincy of John O'Keeffe that he won his first All-Ireland medal when the Sem captured the Hogan Cup, defeating St Mary's of Galway in the final. I had the honour of playing in Croke Park with Paudie when we were members of the Kerry junior team that was defeated in the All-Ireland final in 1969. He was also on the Kerry minor team who lost in the 1970 All-Ireland final, and in 1972 was a member of the Kerry under-21 and senior teams who also lost All-Ireland finals. In fact, Paudie has the rare distinction of having runner-up medals in All-Ireland minor, under-21, junior, senior and also Kerry and Cork senior county championships!

He was blossoming into a great midfielder, and in 1973 was a member of the Kerry under-21 team captained by Mickey Ned O'Sullivan who defeated Mayo in the All-Ireland final. His first taste of senior success came in 1975, when Mick O'Dwyer's young guns overwhelmed a fancied Dublin team; Paudie played a storming game, partnering Pat McCarthy at midfield. In 1976 when the Dubs defeated Kerry in the All-Ireland final he was playing at midfield, but when Kerry next played in an All-Ireland final in 1978, Paudie wore the no. 7 shirt, and in 1980 and 1981 he showed his versatility by winning his last two All-Ireland medals at corner-back.

With his club Beaufort, which he served loyally over the years, he won novice, junior and intermediate county championships; he won a senior county championship with Mid Kerry and a senior Cork championship with UCC. With Kerry he won five All-Ireland senior medals, one All-Ireland under-21 medal, four National leagues and three All-Star awards, with Munster two Railway Cups, with UCC a Sigerson Cup and with St Brendan's Killarney an All-Ireland college medal.

In Paudie Lynch's magnificent career, the media rarely noticed him. He was not a man for the limelight, but his exceptional football ability shone through, and he was a star among stars in that golden era for Kerry football. He was blessed with wonderful skills and everything he did on a pitch had that rare stamp of greatness. In 2011 he was honoured with a Munster Hall of Fame award, a fitting tribute to an exceptional Kerry footballer.

Paudie is a solicitor in Killarney town. Beaufort sits at the foot of Ireland's highest mountain, Carrantuohill. Some other great players that have come out of this little rural club are Kevin and John Coffey, Murt Kelly, Brian Murphy, and of course Paudie's brother, Brendan.

Right half-back: Dr Sean Murphy (Camp)

Without hesitation I include Sean in this Kerry fifteen along with his brother Seamus, whom I picked in the right full-back position: the only two brothers in my selection. I have vivid memories of seeing Sean during the fifties and sixties. I played county championship football against him as he lined out with West Kerry, and indeed opposed him directly when I played in Kerry trials in the early sixties in Killarney. Strong and forceful, a wonderful fielder of the ball, elegant in his movement and blessed with all the skills of the game, so great was he that he was selected by experts in this position on the Team of the Century and the Team of the Millennium.

The 1959 championship decider became known as 'Sean Murphy's All-Ireland final'. His exhibition of Gaelic football that day was reckoned by many to be the finest ever seen in Croke Park. The Irish Texaco Award had been introduced the previous year, and Sean was the first Kerryman to win it. Jack Mahon, centre half-back for Galway in that game, described Murphy's performance to me in an interview as 'Kerry football in all its glory, effortlessly executed by a master'. Here we have a little glimpse into how others perceive the heart and soul of Kerry football.

The late Mick Dunne, one of the doyens of GAA journalists at the time, wrote in the *Irish Press* following that win over Galway:

> When everything else is forgotten about a final which gave Kerry back this supreme football prize ... Sean Murphy's part in it will still be a treasured memory. For the brilliance of the 27-year-old native of Camp sparkled unforgettably in a baffling disappointing final like a rare jewel cast among stones. And his display of magnificent football was so typical of the Kerry power that crushed Galway that he will forever be associated with this latest triumph.

For outsiders it might be difficult to get the small area and the small population of Camp into perspective. Valentia is like a city compared to Camp. Camp is only Camp Cross; there is Ashe's pub, Barry's pub and O'Shea's. Lower Camp, where there is only one house, is half a mile away. In order to play the game of football, the practice in Sean's youth, as he recalled for me, 'was to rent a field from a farmer, whatever field he did not want in that year. The local school played an important part in fostering football ... I went to school at Camp National School, where my mother and my father taught.'

Sean played for the Kerry minors in 1949; they were beaten by Armagh in the final. He was chosen for the juniors and won a junior All-Ireland the same year. To add to his joy, his brother Padraig was also a member of that victorious side. He was young enough to play minor the following year, and Kerry beat Wexford 3–6 to 1–4 in the final. The young boy from Camp had written himself into history's pages by winning a junior All-Ireland medal before he won a minor medal: an amazing accomplishment.

I visited Sean recently in his home in Oakpark, Tralee, where he lives in retirement following a long career in medicine. He recalled his glittering life in the green and gold:

> Essentially I played at right half-back for most of my time with Kerry. In 1953, I started off for Kerry as a sub against Clare. My first playing position was centre-half forward against Cork, whom we defeated in the '53 Munster final. I was taken out of that position to play left half-back against Louth in the semi-final and I was switched to midfield, with Dermot Hannafin as my partner, against Armagh in the All-Ireland final. I won the first of my three All-Ireland senior medals. In 1954 we lost the final to Meath, 1–13 to 1–7. In 1955 I collected my second senior All-Ireland medal when Kerry won 0–12 to 1–6, a victory that shocked Dublin. This was my most special memory.
>
> Kerry was in the doldrums from '56 to '58, but in '59 we came back. Only four of us survived from the '53 team. With me were John Dowling, Paudie Sheehy and Jerome O'Shea. We beat Galway in the final 3–7 to 1–4. Mick O'Connell was captain. We came up against a great Down team in the 1960 final. They won and took the Sam Maguire over the border for the first time. In 1961 Down again beat Kerry in

the semi-final. It was the last of my years in inter-county football. I played from 1949 to 1961 and I was never warned by a referee.

The best teams I played against were Down of 1960 and the Galway team of '59. Cork was always a good team. They played very good football and they were very difficult to beat. We had a theory then that any time you beat Cork you could win an All-Ireland. They were always good enough to test you.

One of the footballers who stands out in my memory as giving the greatest sporting pleasure to his team-mates, the opposition and the spectators was Paddy Doherty of Down. As a back, he was the best player that I ever played against. Another who I rate as first class was Sean Purcell of Galway; he was the best player on the field in my time.

So how good was Dr Sean Murphy? In the *Irish Times* in 1959 following that dazzling display against Galway in the All-Ireland final, Padraig Puirséil, one of my favourite sports writers of the time, wrote of him:

> If I were a Kerryman I think I'd start a subscription to erect a monument to right half-back Sean Murphy from Camp. I'm sure many of the neutral spectators would subscribe, for, on a day when close marking, keen exchanges, and bone hard ground often reduced even long-famed stars into very run-of-the-mill footballers the UCD medical student gave us the most astonishing exhibition of high catching, long kicking, clever anticipation and intelligent passing that I have ever seen in an All-Ireland final. This was a display of sheer class, elegance and style.

Centre-back: Seamus Moynihan (Glenflesk)

I rate Seamus among the five best Kerry footballers I have seen since 1955. He simply had everything required to make him the brilliant, stylish player he was. Just five foot eleven in height, he was a magnificent fielder and had a unique way of weaving and dodging out of danger between opposing players, showing beautiful balance as he left men trailing in his wake. He rarely fouled his opponent and, like all great players, while relying on skill and ability he was also able to mix it with the hardest and toughest of opponents. When St Brendan's College Killarney won the All-Ireland Hogan Cup in 1992, Seamus was the man who dragged them to victory. The same year he went from that school team straight onto the Kerry senior side at midfield: a very rare occurrence. That was the year Clare shocked the Kingdom in the Munster final.

It was the beginning of a magnificent career for the man from the townland of Shronedarraugh in the parish of Glenflesk, halfway between Barraduff and Glenflesk. He played senior with his county from 1992 to 2006, winning every available honour. He also played minor and under-21 for Kerry, appearing in twelve Munster finals and winning eight medals, and appearing in six senior All-Ireland finals and winning four Celtic crosses. Seamus made sixty-one championship appearances for Kerry and ninety-four league appearances. In 2014 he was a selector with the Kerry under-21 team.

During his career with Kerry the team had many ups and downs, and Moynihan was often at his best when Kerry struggled. It was to him that Kerry turned in 2000 when they found themselves without a full-back. Seamus converted overnight from a brilliant wing half-back to a brilliant full-back as Kerry beat Galway in the replayed All-Ireland final. It is rare for a fairly slightly built wing half-back to make this change so successfully. His battles with his friend and former Tralee IT colleague Padraig Joyce were among the highlights of those two finals.

There was a seminal moment in the replay when a long ball was directed towards Joyce, who had sneaked in behind Seamus; had it reached him it could have been catastrophic for Kerry. It did not seem possible for the Kerryman to reach the ball, but somehow he did and danger was averted. In doing so he showed his most valuable trait as a player: the ability to read the play better than anyone around him. This is a hallmark of all great sportsmen, and Moynihan used it to deadly effect over the years. The interceptions he made always seemed easy because he had the knack of being in the right place.

In one way Seamus was unfortunate to be such a versatile player. It meant that he never got an extended spell in his best position at wing-halfback, because when there was a gap to be filled at full-back, corner-back or centre half-back he was always called upon. Indeed, I often felt that midfield would have been his very best position: he could have roamed at will from goal to goal, displaying his wonderful array of skills. Many Kerry people regard matches against Cork as the ultimate test of a Kerry player; the Glenflesk man's performance against the much taller Colin Corkery in a Munster final and a fabulous display at midfield in a league game in the late nineties in Pairc Ui Rinn ensured that he passed that test.

Sometimes success at county level dilutes a player's commitment to his club, but the opposite was the case with Seamus and his beloved Glenflesk. Before he and Johnny Crowley – another Kerry star – came along the club had won the O'Donoghue Cup only once, but Seamus inspired his native place to no fewer than five triumphs in this hotly contested championship, as well as helping East Kerry to three county titles.

Being a great sportsman with recognition all over the country is one thing, but an even greater achievement is being able to carry that greatness with humility and modesty. As the referees of Ireland will testify, Seamus did that on the field. Off the field he has set the standard for all other GAA players to follow in common sense, civility and humility. He lives in Glenflesk with his wife Noreen, son Jamie and daughters Cliona and Eve.

Left half-back: Marc Ó Sé (An Ghaeltacht)

Marc is one of only two of the present generation of Kerry footballers I have chosen for this unique team. The youngest of the three legendary Ó Sé footballing brothers (Darragh and Tomás are the others), Marc is in my opinion the most skilful and graceful when on the ball. While he has played most of his football at corner-back for Kerry, he is equally at home when moved out the field. Indeed, I have often seen him play at centre-forward for his club, and his skill and class shine out wherever he is positioned. He has an amazing dummy when on the ball, and although every opponent is aware that Marc is going to sell this sidestep dummy, they always fall for it.

Marc made his Kerry debut in 2002 under the guidance of his uncle Páidí, and has made over eighty championship appearances in the green and gold. It's rare to see a defender score 0–13 in championship football and 1–7 in league football, but the Gaeltacht man has achieved that. Marc has played minor and under-21 for the county and is the holder of ten Munster medals, five All-Irelands, three National League medals and three All-Star awards.

He has been one of Kerry's most consistent and brilliant defenders over the years, meeting and beating the greatest forwards in the game. He is a natural athlete and never appears to put on even the slightest surplus weight. I have vivid memories of him as a juvenile playing against my club, Killarney Legion, in Kerry juvenile leagues; he stood out as one that was definitely going to play senior for his county. He had sure hands, beautiful movement, that sidestep, ability to dash solo upfield and pinpoint delivery of the ball.

Marc went to university in Maynooth; today he teaches in Tralee CBS and coaches and trains teams there. I will not be one bit surprised if we see him as manager or trainer of a Kerry team.

Centre-field: Mick O'Connell (Valentia Young Islanders)

I have already written about Mick O'Connell in Chapter 9. Probably the most skilful footballer ever to lace a boot, the man from Valentia simply had it all. I consider myself fortunate to have witnessed his skills when he was in his prime, and I have yet to see any player come near his displays at midfield for club and county.

I was on the Kerry panel in 1969 when Mick was playing superb football, and had a close-up view of him both in training and in matches. His classic high fielding, free-kicking, precision passing with both feet and ability to float around opponents will remain etched in the memory. The epitome of that word 'class'.

There was and still is a mystique, a charisma about Mick O'Connell. I love meeting him and chatting about football, as he is always ready to discuss the finer points of the game rather than any of his own memorable performances.

Centre-field: Seanie Walsh (Kerins O'Rahillys)

Seanie won seven All-Ireland medals, four at midfield and three at fullback. Blessed with a fine physique, he stood at six feet one inch and was a pure stylist in everything he did. A magnificent fielder and a beautiful passer of the ball, he possessed a devastating sidestep and could sprint at full pace from a near standing position. Like John O'Keeffe, the Kerins O'Rahillys club man had to retire with a severe hip injury, in 1987. He had a hip replacement in 2002.

Seanie had served his county at senior level from 1976. He won eight Munster medals, seven senior All-Irelands, three National Leagues and two All-Star awards. A magnificent photograph of him by Kerry photographer Kevin Coleman, out-fielding Brian Mullins in Croke Park in 1979 as both reached high for the ball, probably sums him up better than any written word.

In 1975 Kerry won the minor, under-21 and senior All-Irelands. Seanie was at midfield for the first two of those successes – the Kingdom defeated Tyrone 1–10 to 0–4 in the minor decider and Dublin 1–15 to 0–10 in the under-21 final – and became a regular on the senior team later that year. Seeing this strapping Tralee man in action, it was evident to me even then that here was a special talent.

The Kerry under-21 side of that era was one of the greatest ever, packed with men who would go on to become legends of the game. Charlie Nelligan, Páidí Ó Sé, Mick Spillane, Ogie Moran, Sean Walsh, Jack O'Shea, Pat Spillane and Barry Walsh swept to three successive All-Irelands, following the 1975 breakthrough by effortlessly beating Kildare on a scoreline of 0–14 to 1–3 and Down by 1–11 to 1–5 in the '76 and '77 finals. The 1976 final was the first All-Ireland decider to feature the famous Seanie Walsh/Jack O'Shea midfield partnership which would be seen in four senior finals, against Dublin (twice), Roscommon and Offaly.

In an interview with me some years ago Seanie spoke about trainer Mick O'Dwyer:

> We were very lucky that band of players came along at the same time: there were even a lot of excellent players who couldn't get into the county team. Nineteen or twenty players of that era came together and Mick O'Dwyer was a huge influence on our destinies. He kept the

> team together and maintained our discipline. That team would have won one or two All-Irelands, but after that it would have been hard to keep our feet on the ground. Micko did that for us. He kept us keen and hungry. He drove us on to greater heights than we would have dreamed.

Seanie Walsh was the most unselfish of players. He tended to sacrifice his own game, staying around the middle of the pitch while the other midfielder went on runs and availed of the opportunity to look classy. His ball-winning skills were as brilliant as I have seen, and his selflessness contributed hugely to the greater good of the team. I asked him about his partner Jack O'Shea. 'We had a good understanding,' he told me, 'and I enjoyed every minute of playing alongside him. We complemented each other very well – he roamed and I just stayed.'

Seanie has run an auctioneering business in Tralee with Michael O'Sullivan since 1983. He is married to Cork woman Bernadette and they have four children. Two of their sons, Tommy and Barry John, won senior All-Irelands with Kerry in 2009.

Right half-forward: Eamon O'Donoghue (Ballylongford) (RIP)

The younger brother of Paudie O'Donoghue (RIP), Eamon was born in Kilcorman Asdee in the parish of Ballylongford. In 1964, at just eighteen years of age, he was a member of the Shannon Rangers team that won the Kerry senior county championship. I had a close-up of his array of football skills as I was in goal for the defeated East Kerry side that day.

Eamon played Kerry minor for a period, then graduated to the under-21 side and was on the team defeated by Mayo in the 1967 All-Ireland final. He played in goal for Kerry in the senior Munster final of 1967 when the county were defeated by Cork, and was brought out in the closing minutes to help bolster the forward line: Josie O'Brien of Kerins O'Rahillys replaced him in goal. It was the only time in the history of Kerry GAA that such a substitution and positional change was made.

He played in his first senior All-Ireland final in 1968, losing to Down. When Kerry won their twenty-first All-Ireland title in 1969, Eamon wore the no. 12 shirt; he was to play in this position in five All-Ireland finals, including a replay. A beautiful footballer, he could out-jump and out-field taller opponents, was master of the solo run and could take scores with both feet. He had an uncanny ability to read a game and was generally in the right place to take a pass from a colleague or to open up an opposing defence with a well-placed long ball to a fellow attacker. Eamon was a very unselfish player, and often passed to a colleague who was in a better position when he could have scored himself.

He was ahead of his time in that he regularly dropped back in defence to collect kick-outs and link up between backs and forwards. When Mick O'Connell was soaring at midfield, Eamon was moving into position to accept a long foot pass. His understanding with O'Connell was a feature of Kerry's great victories in that period.

Eamon won his second senior All-Ireland medal in 1970 when Kerry defeated Meath in the final. As a club player he had few equals: with O'Rahillys of Ballylongford he won three Kerry Intermediate championships and five North Kerry senior championships. With Shannon Rangers he won three All-Ireland seven-a-side championships and three Kerry senior county championships. With Kerry he won two senior All-Ireland medals and five National leagues, and with Munster one Railway Cup medal.

Eamon O'Donoghue was more than just a marvellous player; his sportsmanship, commitment and unassuming demeanour represented everything that is positive and enriching in the great game of Gaelic football. When Ballylongford qualified to play Moyvane in the 1970 Glin Tournament final, the match was fixed for the same evening as Kerry's Munster final against Cork. Paudie and Eamon helped Kerry to win the Munster crown and then arrived in Glin still in their gear; they played a huge part in Bally's victory.

I had the pleasure of playing with and against Eamon and training with him as we prepared for All-Ireland finals, and roomed with him on our world tour in 1970. A quiet, private, courteous person, he expressed himself on the football field.

A teacher by profession, Eamon sadly died a very young man on 7 March 1983. The North Kerry Championship Cup is named in his honour.

Centre-forward: Pat Griffin (Glenbeigh/Glencar/Clonakilty, Co. Cork)

Another supreme stylist, Pat was well before his time and his speedy, jinking runs as he sold dummies all over the place played a huge part in helping Kerry to the All-Ireland wins of 1969 and 1970. With superb balance, he relied entirely on his skills to beat his opponent and I am convinced that he could take his place on any Kerry team of the modern era.

On Kerry's world tour of 1970 I was playing in goal as Pat received a serious back injury against the Aussies in Wagga Wagga. This seriously affected his career. Now a retired Garda in Clonakilty, Pat played with Kerry from 1963 to 1973, making eighty-four league and championship appearances and scoring a total of 6 goals and 77 points. He played in six All-Ireland senior finals and was on the winning side twice.

Pat was born in the Kingdom; his family moved to Kildare when he was seven years of age. He played football with the Clane club and for the Kildare minors and seniors. In 1963 the family moved to Killorglin. He told me: 'It was a bit of a wrench leaving Kildare. I had been very happy there, but at the end of the day was always a Kerryman. I played football for Glenbeigh, the club from where we originally lived in Glencar.'

Pat performed in midfield and in the forward line, but is best remembered for his brilliance on the forty. He lined out for Mid Kerry, a divisional side, in senior competition, and will never forget his competitive debut for the Kingdom. 'I was brought on as a sub in the 1963 Munster Final [in which Kerry beat Cork 1–18 to 3–7]. It was a great thrill to come on in front of forty or fifty thousand people, especially when I was lining out with the likes of Mick O'Connell, Mick O'Dwyer and Tom Long, men who had been my heroes. When I was young I'd go out to the field kicking the ball and pretend I was one of them. All of a sudden, here I was playing on the county team with them!'

Pat joined the Garda in 1965 and was posted to Clonakilty three years later. He was on the Kerry under-20 side that won the first All-Ireland in that grade in 1964: 'We beat Laois [1–10 to 1–3] in a tough game in Croke Park.' As captain, Pat led Kerry all the way to the All-Ireland final in 1968, only to be defeated by Down.

His memories of his final years in the green and gold are vivid. 'I played in the Munster final in '71 and got knocked out; I was back for the '72 All-Ireland final when Offaly beat us in a replay. I opted out in '73 [at just twenty-nine years of age] but was asked back with Mick O'Connell for the '74 Munster final. We were subs that day when Cork beat us [1–11 to 0–7]. I slipped out of the scene totally after that.'

Pat Griffin's inter-county career was over. Many say he is one of the forgotten men of Kerry football: another quiet and extremely courteous man, he was for me one of the first of the great Kerry stylists. To have trained with him and played with and against him are memories that I will never forget.

Left half-forward: Tadghie Lyne (Dr Crokes) (RIP)

In 1955 Tadghie Lyne, trained and coached by Dr Eamonn O'Sullivan, helped power Kerry to All-Ireland victory over Dublin in a final that is still spoken of as one of the best ever.

Tadghie, blessed with all the skills of the game, gave one of the greatest displays of point-kicking that day. Maurice Fitzgerald in 1997 was for me reminiscent of that exhibition.

The very mention of his name evokes a multitude of memories. When I was growing up in Killarney in the 1950s he was my first real-life sporting hero: superbly fit, tall and rangy, dark hair slicked back, kicking points from all distances and angles. A glance at the goalposts was all he needed before kicking his trademark high, arcing point: a skill perfected over many hours of practice in Fitzgerald Stadium and at his father's garage in High Street, Killarney. What an honour it was to act as ball-boy to the great man as he practised.

Tadghie Lyne won an All-Ireland basketball medal with Kerry in 1957; he was also a star at pitch and putt, snooker, billiards and athletics, and represented Munster and Ireland in football. He won senior All-Ireland medals in 1953, 1955 and 1959.

Tadghie – a quiet, shy person – on one occasion acquiesced to an interview request, and I found myself in his home for my Radio Kerry *Terrace Talk* show. This interview, in retrospect, is a vital record in the history of Kerry football, because it is the only available discussion with one of Kerry's greatest ever footballers: the man fittingly hailed as the Prince of Forwards.

He was born in Sunnyhill, Killarney, one of three boys and two girls. His mother was Nellie Flynn from Firies; his father Jerome was a Kilgarvan man and, as Tadghie recalled, 'played a bit of hurling'. He attended school at the Presentation Monastery and St Brendan's College, where his football powers were soon noticed. He did not get in the Kerry minor side of his year but he did help the Sem to win two Dunloe Cups and a Munster Championship. He told me:

> I started playing with the Killarney minors at left half-back. It was okay but I loved the forwards, and my favourite position was left half-forward. Eamon was a great trainer and Paul Russell was with him for the 1955 final ... We were staying in St Brendan's College that year, and before the Cavan semi-final a gang of us decided we would go to Puck Fair for the night. About fourteen of us went in a lorry and the following day we got a fierce gruelling.
>
> Eamon was all about sprinting because 'get the ball first' was his motto. I was at my peak in that 1955 final; I scored the first point, getting the ball from the late John Dowling. It was great just to beat Dublin alone; however, my fondest memory is the first All-Ireland I won in 1953 against Armagh. I was all nerves at the start and wanted to come off, but Eamon told Colm Kennelly and Donie Murphy to play the ball to me and I got a few catches and I settled down. Bill McCorry missed the penalty, I don't remember much more, but that was my favourite memory.

Tadghie's distinctive style of kicking was like Maurice Fitzgerald, Pat Spillane and Mikey Sheehy rolled into one. I asked him how he became so accurate.

> Every evening when the garage closed I would hang two footballs off the rafters with ropes about three inches from the ground, and hit them with my left and right legs, trapping them as they swung back. I would do that for about an hour every night until I perfected my style. I would have the follow-through to precision; it is the follow-through that that makes the kick. If you don't follow through, the ball can go anywhere, so that's how I did it. I also practised putting spin on the ball to the left or right; this is very difficult to do but you get used to it after lots of practice and I used it a lot in my career.

The Killarney man was Kerry's top scorer in 1955, 1956 and 1959, while his total for Kerry in 1955 was 5–42 (57 points) in fourteen games: an average of 4.07 points per game, fantastic kicking in any man's language. Tadghie Lyne was for me the first superstar of Kerry football, with the style, class, skill, bravery, deadly accuracy and modesty that I now realise are an integral part of all the men I have chosen for this Kerry fifteen.

Although he had been in deteriorating health for some time, his death at his home on Killarney Road, Castleisland on 31 May 2000 came as a great shock to his family and huge circle of friends and admirers. He was sixty-nine years old.

Right corner-forward: Mike Sheehy (Austin Stacks)

'Nureyev with a football': Gabriel Fitzmaurice's poem about Mike Sheehy sums up his genius and shows how he is regarded by all followers of the game. The Austin Stacks man made his debut with the senior team in a league match against Roscommon in Tralee on 8 October 1973, which Kerry won. He is famous as one of the golden era team of 1975–86, winning eight All-Ireland medals. Mike played at full-forward in the 1975 final when an unfancied young team of bachelors easily defeated All-Ireland champions Dublin. He was free-taker and, for a man of twenty-one years, showed remarkable composure.

The 1978 final is remembered above all for the goal Mike scored against Paddy Cullen in the latter stages of the first half. Dublin had been dominant but a breakaway goal by John Egan brought Kerry back into the game. An altercation between Ger Power and Paddy Cullen resulted in referee Seamus Aldridge awarding Kerry a dubious free on the 14 yard line, at an angle to the goal on the Hogan Stand side. Cullen argued with Aldridge about the free. The quick-thinking Mike placed the ball and, seeing that the Dublin goal was unoccupied, chipped it over the retreating goalkeeper's head into the net and into history. Con Houlihan wrote that 'Paddy dashed back towards his goal like a woman who smells a cake burning ... The ball won the race and it curled inside the near post as Paddy crashed into the outside of the net and lay against it like a fireman who had returned to find his station ablaze.'

The following year, Mike scored 2–6 in Kerry's win over Dublin. In 1980 he pounced for the vital goal in a very tight match against Roscommon. In 1981 he provided the final pass for Jack O'Shea's goal against Offaly which sealed the four-in-a-row. But the five-in-a-row was agonisingly denied by Offaly in 1982.

Kerry came back to win three in a row. Mike missed the 1984 final but was present for the victories in 1985 and 1986. In 1987, he scored his second most famous goal when he wriggled through the clutches of several Cork defenders to give Kerry the lead in the last minutes of the Munster final. But Cork equalised, and the glory era was comprehensively ended the following Sunday in Killarney: a day when Mike's scoring boots went missing. The following spring, on medical advice, he announced his retirement.

Thus ended one of the most distinguished careers in the history of Kerry football. Along with eight senior All-Irelands went two under-21 All-Irelands, eleven Munster titles, three Leagues, seven All-Stars, four Kerry titles and a club All-Ireland with Stacks, as well as selection on the Centenary and Millennium teams.

However, Mike will be remembered for his style of play as much as for the honours he gained. He danced around the field, eluding his marker, gliding into empty spaces, always in the right place at the right time. He could side-step; he could swerve. He had an astonishing ability to chip the ball up into his hands when running at speed, even on a wet day. His understanding with his teammates was telepathic; he blossomed especially when Eoin Liston became the target man from 1978 onwards. The full-forward line of Sheehy, Liston, Egan was undoubtedly the best in the history of the GAA.

He scored points from impossible angles. On one occasion he scored a point on the half volley, letting a cross-field pass from Pat Spillane hop in front of him before drawing on it and sending it over the bar. It all seemed effortless with Mike. His free-taking was immaculate, any free within 50 yards an almost certain point for Kerry. Pressure brought out the best in him: he loved taking frees into the Hill.

Above all, he was a sportsman. Never involved in controversy, a gentleman on and off the field, he was extremely modest about his talent. When interviewed, he made it appear as if luck had favoured him. But there was little luck involved: there was skill and ability and genius.

Full-forward: Maurice Fitzgerald (St Mary's, Caherciveen)

Mention this name wherever GAA followers are gathered and the response will be unanimous: he was one of the greatest we have seen. I was fortunate to see this wonderful player in action all through his career with his club, South Kerry district and of course with Kerry. His senior career lasted from 1988 to 2001; he made 107 appearances for his county, scoring 23 goals and 442 points. He played in twelve Munster finals, winning six, and won All-Ireland medals in the only two final appearances he made, in 1997 and 2000.

Maurice Fitzgerald toiled for ten years on a Kerry team that played second fiddle to Cork (no back door to the championship then). For most of those years he was to a large extent our only sustenance. On dreary October/November days he brightened our lives with the grandeur of his artistry and cajoled us into believing that summer days would come again. Come again they did in 1997, when Maurice turned in the greatest individual display I have ever seen by any Gaelic footballer. He scored 0–9 as the Kingdom won by 0–13 to 1–7, and afterwards the game was dubbed 'the Maurice Fitzgerald final'.

Wizardry with the ball allied to the movement of a ballet dancer made the Caherciveen man stand out among all others on view. His skills were simply awesome and, as we saw in that 1997 All-Ireland final win over Mayo, he could appear as if he was from a different world. Yet his pre-match build up was not something that any sports scientist would be too happy with.

Fitzgerald told me in one of the many interviews we conducted that he would often miss team training in Killarney the week of a final, and instead would stick to his own routine in his home town.

> These lads would be getting very excited above in Killarney and if I went up I'd be listening to this kip o' the reel from all of them and it would tire me out. I couldn't be listening to all this joking around. I needed a bit of time out. So I used to go for a few cones with my great friend Kieran McCarthy down in Caherciveen.

> The idea of going up and down for two hours didn't really appeal to me and in fairness, a lot of it would have been chit-chat and I felt I wanted to hone down on getting my kicking right and things like that. I was probably doing a bit of fine-tuning. Or else I was gone for a 99.

That was Maurice: an easy-going, different approach. The Kerry football pedigree is certainly there. Maurice's father Ned was a Kerry captain in the late 1950s, while Seamus O'Connor (a brother of Mary, his late mother) is the holder of a record ten South Kerry Championship medals.

In 1990, accompanied by his father, Maurice travelled to Australia where he defeated an Australian rugby player, a Rules player and an Aussie soccer starlet in a free-taking world challenge in Melbourne. Fitzgerald was equally brilliant off left or right leg, from frees or open play: a rarity in the game today.

Living in his home town of Caherciveen and married with three children, Maurice teaches in Coláiste na Sceilge, and has continued to play with his club up to the present day. His took to management recently and guided St Mary's to an intermediate All-Ireland final victory in Croke Park in 2015.

Left corner-forward: Colm Cooper (Dr Crokes)

Colm 'Gooch' Cooper is one of the most talented forwards to come out of Killarney since Dick Fitzgerald. Just as Dick dominated Kerry football in the first decade and a half of the twentiethth century, winning five All-Irelands, his natural successor Colm Cooper has been the dominant figure 100 years later, with four All-Irelands so far and unlucky not to have more.

Colm emerged onto the senior team in 2002 at the age of eighteen. His reputation had preceded him, but it was easy to have doubts. He was slim and slight, weighing around ten stone. In his street clothes, he looked frail and vulnerable. How could this youngster survive against teak-tough backs like Kieran McGeeney and Francie Bellew of Armagh, and Darren Fay of Meath?

We got an answer. In his Kerry jersey, it was so different. The backs were unable to lay a hand on him. Colm Cooper proved to be one of the best corner-forwards – arguably the best – that the game has seen. His speed of movement and of thought was far ahead of any of his opponents, and often of his teammates. Despite his apparent frailty, he was six feet in height and well able to win a fifty-fifty ball sent in his direction. He then had an amazing ability to create space, to have time on the ball. He was always looking for a goal: a point was only the second option.

He had all the skills. Perhaps the most distinctive was his dummy hop, which fooled defenders time and again. When in possession and under pressure, he could hop the ball, throwing it a little too far in front of him – or so it seemed. As his marker dived in to take possession, the ball would bounce back like a yo-yo into Colm's hands, the marker would be left grasping at thin air and Colm had time and space either to score himself or to create a score for a teammate.

He was elusive; he had the swerve, the twists and turns, the bewildering changes of direction, the flicks and tricks, the dummy solos, the chip-up pick-up. Marking him must have been like marking mercury.

Colm's first game for Kerry was in a Division 2 League final against Laois when he scored a goal in the first minutes. More famous scores were to follow. Who can forget the goal against Mayo in the 2004 final, the fisted goal against Cork in the 2007 final, the goal against Dublin in the first minute of the 2009 quarter-final, the six pointed frees against Cork in that year's final, mostly for fouls on himself? There were many other great scores through the years, for Kerry and for Dr Crokes, whom he inspired to four county championships in a row between 2010 and 2013.

2013 saw Colm in a new role as he moved from the corner to centre-forward. Although Kerry were to lose the shoot-out, Colm gave a master class in the semi-final against Dublin, his vision, creation of space and accurate kick-passing leading to many of Kerry's scores.

In February 2014 Colm suffered a cruciate injury in the club semi-final which ruled him out for the entire year. There was despair and gloom in Kerry and, in fairness, disappointment throughout the entire country that his genius would not be on display. As Kerry battled to an unlikely All-Ireland title, Colm remained part of the panel, although unable to play. Kieran Donaghy gave him the credit for Donaghy's vital goal in the final against Donegal, when he said that Colm's voice came into his head when he was one-on-one with the Donegal goalkeeper: 'Don't blast it – pass it to the net' – which he did.

Tomás Ó Sé, in his recent book, says 'Gooch is the best I've seen.' Paul Galvin describes his 'innate unorthodoxy': 'He has this cold composure. He sees things differently and unconventionally … In sport, this is called genius.'

Colm is a footballing genius: one of the best forward I have seen. He has played in nine All-Ireland finals, winning four; he has eight All-Star awards. But he has remained humble and approachable. In his role as ambassador for AIB, he has travelled the country giving coaching sessions in schools and youth groups, always impressing with his soft-spoken modesty.

13

REMEMBERING KERRY LEGENDS

Kerry honours and remembers its footballers in unique ways: and why not, with all that history, tradition and success since the foundation of the GAA? Bronze statues; roads, roundabouts, football stadiums, even football teams themselves all called after Kerry heroes. Wherever you go in the county, footballing success permeates the air; it arises in conversation wherever you travel; it's all around you: it engulfs you. On my journeys around Kerry I am struck by the real heart and soul of Kerry football and the massive impact it has on its people.

When All-Ireland fever is at its peak and when Kerry are battling it out in the final stages of the championship, the real spirit, the secret of Kerry, the wonder, the marvel of what it all means to its people is unveiled. Family, football and religion: in my opinion it's in that order that most Kerry people view life in the Kingdom, and really it is a form of brainwashing because from birth every child finds reminders wherever they travel of the county's greatness and history.

Since the Sam Maguire Cup first came to Kerry in 1929, thousands of babies and young children were placed inside it to have had their photograph taken. The giant cup is in constant demand in the county, it has its own diary in the county board offices and it has graced baptisms, marriages and deaths, socials and banquets. When it travels outside the country it has its own seat on the plane, and, as I have witnessed, when it visits New York, Boston, London or Chicago the Kerry diaspora line up in their hundreds to have their photograph taken with it.

In the run-up to All-Ireland finals shop windows are adorned with footballs, photographs of players and teams; old newspapers recounting the triumphs of the past are on display wherever you go; songs are written eulogising players past and present. It's the handing down of tradition, reminding everyone of where they come from and of the new generation chasing the glories of those who went before them. I know of one lifelong follower of Kerry who warned his family that when he died, instead of prayers from a priest at his graveside, a Kerry footballer was to be asked to recite the wonderful Kerry football poem, 'You Asked What's the Secret of Kerry'. His dying wish was granted in 2015.

I believe that one of the true secrets of Kerry is that the traditions and love for its footballers are nurtured in its schools. I know from my own experience as a pupil in the Presentation Monastery that when the cup visits a school, it has a great impression on young minds. With so many All-Ireland victories, such visits have had a greater impact on young people in Kerry than in other counties, with the exception of course of Kilkenny and its magnificent hurling success.

In June 2012, I was in Waterville to attend the unveiling of a bronze statue of one of Kerry's greatest sons: Mick O'Dwyer, player, trainer and manager, and the first Kerry footballer to have a statue erected in his honour.

It's rare to be still alive and honoured in this way. It's a beautiful work of art by London-born sculptor Alan Hall, who told me in an interview: 'I had a problem choosing the final pose and eventually what we settled on is one from O'Dwyer's playing days, ball in hand, driving forward, socks rolled down around the ankles, looking forward for a teammate, total concentration.' Alan worked from a photograph taken from O'Dwyer's authorised biography written by his great friend the late Owen McCrohan in 1990.

It's a stunning pose and, having played with and against Micko, for me it captures him exactly as I remember him: one of the five best Kerry footballers I have seen. Behind the statue is a curved wall on which seven plaques of Valentia slate list his achievements (though not all – otherwise the wall would stretch from Waterville to Killarney).

The unveiling was done by then Minster for Arts, Heritage and the Gaeltacht Jimmy Deenihan, who played under Mick. A stone's throw from this statue is one of Charlie Chaplin, who holidayed regularly in Waterville in the forties and fifties, also by Alan Hall.

Mick O'Dwyer, the Waterville wizard, immortalised in bronze. No man deserved it more.

14

KERRY SUPPORTERS: A DIFFERENT BREED

The Kerry Supporters' Club is an intrepid group of men and women: hail, rain or snow they are on the road following their beloved Kerry football teams. They always see the glass as half full and are forever looking forward to the next match, the next journey, the glorious summer victories just around the corner.

They are a massive part of the heart and soul of Kerry football, the real grass roots of the organisation in the county; their lives, families and work revolve around Kerry football. To spend time in their company is a humbling experience.

I was fortunate to spend time in the company of these men and women – and indeed a fair few children – in March 2016. The Four Seasons Hotel is in Coolshannagh, Monaghan town, just thirty minutes' drive from Clones, where Kerry defeated Monaghan on 27 March in the National League. This was chosen as base camp for the two busloads of supporters from the Kingdom. Garry O'Sullivan and I were on Radio Kerry duty for the game and we spent the Saturday evening and Sunday morning with the supporters' club. It was a delightful experience.

Over 100 supporters – young and old, men and women – sat down to dinner at 7.30 p.m., and of course conversation centred entirely on football. The troubles of the country and even the world in general were put on hold. It was a wonderful evening of Kerry football education, and during long debates any mistaken date, a wrong score or even selection of your greatest ever Kerry player would be swiftly challenged.

Not all supporters travel on the buses; many with young children travel by car but are booked in for the meal with the supporters. Officers Donie O'Leary (chairman), John King (secretary) and Martin Leane (PRO) are on hand to ensure that everything is spot-on. Music, chat and song will be heard long into the night. People like Jerry Brosnan, Dan Dwyer, Christina Casey, Ann and Ted Regan, Eimear Hogan, Bernie Broderick, John Creedon, the late Kate Clifford from Ballyduff and others too numerous to mention typify the true Kerry supporter.

Jerry Brosnan from Moyvane, now in his eighties, is the senior member of the club; he has a football pedigree second to none. His father, the legendary Con Brosnan, won six All-Irelands in the twenties and thirties; his brother Dr Jim won two All-Irelands and was chairman of the Kerry county board. When Jerry talks, football people listen. The handing down of tradition is very evident here.

It's impossible to say with certainty who has been Kerry's greatest supporter, but a lady from Caherciveen would be well in the running: Kathleen O'Sullivan, affectionately known as 'Small Kathleen', has followed Kerry and Kerry clubs all her life and has attended every final played by Kerry teams in Croke Park since 1971.

But back to my weekend with the Kerry Supporters' Club. The foyer of the Four Seasons Hotel on the Sunday morning of the match is a hive of activity.

It's the meeting point for all: the previous night's singers are openly discussed with great humour; football discussions continue to rage; Sunday newspaper sports sections are browsed through; Brian Sheehan's absence is a major topic – who will be the team's free-kicker? Tthe weather is another big talking point; anxious eyes scan the darkening clouds. Long-serving Mike Allen from Fries sets minds at ease around a crowded table: 'Don't worry about the weather – Kerry can win in any conditions.'

Sunday mass is a top priority for many; taxis ferry supporters to and from St Macartan's Cathedral. As time ticks on, you can sense the excitement beginning to build; watches put forward an hour that morning are constantly checked and mobile phones are buzzing. Martin Leane gently steers his charges to the buses. Clones is reached in loads of time and the Creighton Hotel in Fermanagh Street is commandeered as a second base: standing room only, soup and sandwiches are the order of the day. Now it just a five minute walk up the hilly street to St Tiernach's Park.

I meet Ann Marie O'Sullivan, Birmingham born, just flown in from that city. Her father was a renowned Killarney boat man, Mickey 'Cut' O Sullivan. He instilled in her a love for Kerry football. 'I just love mixing with these wonderful Kerry supporters: their passion is infectious', she tells me.

Former Kerry player and selector Kevin Griffin, with Bernie O'Riordan and others, arrives at the hotel to join the discussion; they left their homes at 7 a.m. Kevin's lovely son Cathal has travelled with the supporters and informs his father that he is not travelling home with him in his car, because 'There is a far better *craic* in the supporters' bus.' Kevin and Bernie laugh heartily at this.

Long before throw-in the centre of the main stand is taken over by the Kerry supporters. They are within touching distance of Garry and me in our commentary position. I find their presence very reassuring for some reason:

it's home from home, friendly faces, green and gold, waving, smiling, chatting, laughing, anxious, passing messages for friends at home and around the world to be called out on the radio. Great stuff. I have experienced the passion, pride and commitment of Kerry's supporters since I first saw the county play in the Munster final of 1955 in Killarney. If anything their numbers have doubled.

And so to the match. The supporters stand as one when Aidan O'Mahony leads out his Kerry team (the Rathmore warrior will play a blinder). They are in great voice and join in as the National Anthem is beautifully sung by fourteen-year-old All-Ireland champion Katie Boyle. And Eamonn Fitzmaurice and his men give them something special to discuss on the long road home. The teams are level at six points apiece at the short whistle, and the second half passes in a flash. Kieran Donaghy has his best game for a long time as he ranges from goal to goal, Colm Cooper is back to his best, selling dummies all over the place, and the supporters are furious when he is refused a penalty in the first half. David Moran, Johnny Buckley and Shane Enright, and indeed all the players and subs introduced, turn on a superb display. Each high catch, block down, perfect pass and score is cheered to the echo: Kerry football for Kerry supporters far from home at its scintillating best.

They hold their breath when Paul Murphy is hauled to the ground and Kerry are awarded a penalty. David Moran expertly goals from the spot; hats, flags and hands are in the air. Kerry are coasting: fresh, fit, all movement. Monaghan are shattered. The supporters are in great voice: someone begins a verse of 'Happy Days Are Here Again'. Kerry are now pushing up on Rory Beggan's kick-outs and the game's dynamic changes completely. Paul Murphy, Colm Cooper, Alan Fitzgerald and Kieran 'Star' Donaghy all raise white flags within minutes: real Kerry points, class and style, seven players on the scoring list, ruthless efficiency. Pride is bursting out all over. Eamonn Fitzmaurice's half-time talk has worked wonders.

A lovely touch: as each Kerry player runs off to be substituted the supporters stand, whistle, shout and applaud. Then the full-time whistle: a 1–17 to 1–9 win. Many of the delighted supporters walk on the field: smiles as wide as the mouth of the Shannon; happy days are here again. Photographs, autographs, selfies, chatting with their heroes, reluctant to head for the bus. Eamonn leaves the dressing room, boards the buses, thanks and praises the supporters. A class act. This is the icing on the cake.

The mood will be buoyant on the long journey home. Expert and critical analysis, more singing, football quiz questions, debates, the future: they are one family for this weekend, following in the footsteps of thousands gone before; knowledgeable, contented, exemplary Kerry people, and the salt of the earth. My kind of people.

Another pit stop for a meal at An Poitín Stil just outside Dublin, then the road home to their beloved Kingdom. For the Kerry Supporters' Club there is always another journey, bad days and good days. Their friendship, welcome and courtesy always leaves me with that warm glow of something special.

The diehard Kerry supporter looks forward to the travels of the league but even more to the summer championship run. His holiday plans must fit into the GAA schedule: the couple of weeks abroad must always be taken when there is a clear gap between matches (and possible replays must be allowed for).

The dedicated Kerry supporter is not an 'animal', as affectionately described by former manager Páidí Ó Sé, but informed, reflective, certainly critical at times, but basically supportive of the manager and team. Nor does he have the 'We'll wait for the final' attitude of previous generations. You asked what's the secret of Kerry? Must be its supporters.

EPILOGUE: MEMORIALS

On 16 May 2015 I made the journey to West Kerry, along the winding road that skirts the wild Atlantic Ocean: stunning scenery, crashing waves and fuchsia-covered hedgerows. No place like it in the world. My destination was Ard a Bhothair in Ventry for the unveiling of a memorial bronze statue to the man known affectionately to one and all as PO.

Páidí Ó Sé, who won eight All-Ireland medals as a player and guided his county to two as a manager, died suddenly on 15 December 2012, aged fifty-seven. On the day that would have been his sixtieth birthday, hundreds of friends, former teammates from near and far and, of course, family gathered to remember the Kerry legend.

His likeness and the iconic no. 5 jersey that he wore with such pride for his beloved Kerry have been captured in bronze outside his well-known pub in Ventry. The piece was commissioned by the Páidí Ó Sé Monument Committee, which formed in 2014 to perpetuate the memory of the Ventry man who achieved extraordinary things for county, district and parish.

Clare sculptor Séamus Connolly was commissioned to create the statue and is no stranger to honouring GAA legends, having won acclaim for his statues of Dermot Earley (Roscommon) and Mick Mackey (Limerick). As he explained to me, it was not an easy task.

> It is exciting and very daunting at the same time ... and indeed terrifying to be handed the responsibility. Having spent several months researching Páidí and his career, I wanted to capture the exact image of the man and I hope I have achieved this. It is slightly larger than life, it's mounted on a beautiful piece of Valentia slate and it depicts Páidí when he was in his early twenties and at the height of his football powers.

For me Séamus has captured the real spirit and lasting image of the great man exactly as I remember him. It's a stunning piece of work: Páidí, with his tremendous physique and will to win, charging upfield, ball balanced in his left hand as was his trademark when in full flight. It was a poignant moment for the huge crowd when his former manager Mick O'Dwyer pulled the cord that unveiled the statue.

Páidí's image is sure to inspire and motivate young Kerry boys and girls to emulate their heroes. As I have said, this is what Kerry is all about: the handing down of tradition; new generations of footballers chasing the dreams of those who have gone before them. It's a never-ending story.

As you drive into Tralee, at the Clashlehane roundabout, an unusual sculpture meets the eye: four figures, two on the alert as two others jump high; one, undoubtedly a Kerryman, grasping the ball – maybe Mick O'Connell, maybe Darragh Ó Sé, or Tralee's own Sean Walsh in a duel with Dublin's Brian Mullins. This sculpture, by Mark Rode, is your introduction to Tralee; it defines a county that has won thirty-seven All-Ireland senior football titles and a town that holds more All-Ireland medals than any other.

The medals first came when Kerry, captained by Tralee corner-forward Tady Gorman, won the 1903 All-Ireland, and have accumulated with every victory up to 2009, when another Tralee corner-forward, Tommy Walsh, scored four crucial points in the win over Cork.

En route to the John Joe Sheehy Road, you pass the Joe Keohane roundabout. Joe, another John Mitchels hero and an uncompromising full-back, was part of the three-in-a-row team from 1939 to 1941; he won a total of five All-Ireland medals and played in the Polo Grounds All-Ireland. Joe remained a part of Kerry football for many decades and was one of Mick O'Dwyer's right-hand men behind the great team of the 1970s.

As you move into the town and turn for the station, you drive along the John Joe Sheehy Road. An icon of Kerry football, a forward with speed, skill and accuracy, John Joe captained Kerry to success in 1926 and 1930. In 1924, while he still was on the run after the Civil War, a safe passage to enable him to play in matches was arranged by Con Brosnan, midfielder and Free State army captain. John Joe retired suddenly in the summer of 1931 when he felt that his speed was deserting him. He remained active in Kerry GAA as a selector and was president of the county board when he died. He created a football dynasty, as three of his sons also won All-Ireland medals. It is fitting that the road named after him passes the clubhouse of his old team, John Mitchels, and runs up to Austin Stack Park, headquarters of Kerry GAA.

Near the centre of town is the Jackie Power roundabout. Jackie, a Limerick man who won two All-Ireland hurling medals with his own county, settled in Tralee in the early 1950s. He trained the Kerry hurlers to win the 1961 junior All-Ireland and in 1973 achieved an extraordinary training double: Limerick to win the hurling All-Ireland and Austin Stacks to win the Kerry football championship. His son Ger won eight All-Ireland medals.

On the western side of Tralee is the Dan Spring Road, called after the O'Rahillys man who played for Kerry from 1934 till 1940. He starred in the

1939 win over Meath, scoring 2–2 of Kerry's total of 2–5. Dan captained Kerry to win the 1940 All-Ireland, the first Strand Road man to do so. He was injured early in the second half of that game and it was his last match for Kerry. Some years later, he was elected to the Dáil as a Labour Party TD and enjoyed a long and successful political career.

Near the racecourse is the Bill Kinnerk Road. Bill was a John Mitchels clubman who played mainly at corner-back for Kerry, won an All-Ireland medal in 1937, was captain in 1938 when Kerry lost the final to Galway in a replay and later became a local councillor.

The most recent road to be called after a footballer is the Bracker O'Regan Road. This honours Austin Stacks' Martin O'Regan, called 'the Bracker' by all. An active, lively man into his nineties, he was a regular in the bookies' offices and at Tralee greyhound track having his daily bet. It was Bracker who replaced John Joe Sheehy when he retired suddenly in the summer of 1931. He scored three goals in that first game, a Munster final against Tipperary, went on to win an All-Ireland and was the oldest medallist in Kerry at the time of his death in 2005, aged ninety-five.

Two great Kerry footballers are commemorated at either end of the Bracker O'Regan Road. The Mounthawk roundabout is dedicated to Joe Barrett, from Austin Stacks, holder of six All-Ireland medals. One of the great Kerry full-backs, he captained Kerry in 1929 and 1932 and famously, in a magnanimous gesture, handed over his right to the captaincy in 1931 to Con Brosnan, who had served Kerry football well but whose club was unlikely ever to win the county championship. The Monavalley roundabout is dedicated to another Austin Stacks player from a famous footballing family, John Joe 'Purty' Landers, a forward who was part of the four-in-a-row team and won another medal in 1937.

The P.P. Fitzgerald roundabout at one end of the Dan Spring Road commemorates one of the founding fathers of the Strand Road club, Kerins O'Rahillys, and the Kevin Barry roundabout at the top of Rock Street honours a former Austin Stacks and Kerry footballer.

So, Tralee honours its GAA players in a way that is unique for an Irish town. And there is room for more: with a ring road being constructed, the councillors of the county have an opportunity to honour additional players. Perhaps John Dowling, captain of the 1955 team; maybe Dan O'Keeffe, long-serving goalkeeper and holder of seven All-Ireland medals, or some of those happily still with us: John O'Keeffe, stylish full-back or Mike Sheehy, scorer extraordinaire.

It is right and fitting that these GAA heroes are remembered in their home place. In Tralee, the great players from the past won't be forgotten.

INDEX OF NAMES

A

Ahern, Pat 67
Aldridge, Seamus 212
Allen, Denis 21, 106
Allen, Mike 223

B

Barrett, Jack 131
Barrett, Joe 66, 126–7, 228
Barrett, John 41, 42, 45
Barrett, Tim 41, 42
Barron, Declan 105–6
Barry, Dave 106
Barry, John 193
Barry, Kevin 230
Barry-Murphy, Jimmy 21, 81, 196
Beggan, Rory 224
Behan, Billy 79
Bellew, Francie 216
Bernard, Denis 106
Bowler, Teddy 67, 154
Boyle, Katie 224
Bradley, Mark 124
Breen, Maurice 38
Breen, Mick 154
Bridgeman, Tommy 144
Broderick, Bernie 222
Brogan, Alan 113, 114
Brogan, Bernard (Jr) 114
Brogan, Bernard (Sr) 111
Brosnan, Bridie 179
Brosnan, Con 25, 126, 222, 228, 229
Brosnan, Eoin 118
Brosnan, Jerry 222
Brosnan, Jim 47, 65, 138
Brosnan, Kathleen 181
Brosnan, Mike 15, 24
Brosnan, Liam 100
Brosnan, Noel 100
Brosnan, Paddy Bawn 25, 42, 128
Buckley, Johnny 224
Bunyan, John 67, 144
Bunyan, Robert 144
Burrows, Seanie 67
Busby, Matt 11, 79, 80

C

Cahalane, Niall 106
Callaghan, Colm 67
Canavan, Peter 119, 120
Cantillon, Paul 38
Carey, Jarlath 53
Carr, Barney 49, 50
Carr, Tom 112
Carvin, Jack 'Sandman' 60
Casey, Bill 25
Casey, Christina 222
Casey, Willie Joe 22
Cavanagh, Dan 173
Cavanagh, Seán 119
Chaplin, Charlie 220
Cleary, Sean 42
Clifford, Kate 222
Clifford, Michael 32
Cluxton, Stephen 114
Cody, Brian 155
Coffey, John 196
Coffey, Kevin 196
Coffey, Pats 33
Colbert, Moss 46
Coldrick, David 121
Coleman, John 106
Coleman, Kevin 15, 204
Collins, Amelia 181
Collins, Tom 38, 41, 42
Connolly, Diarmuid 112–13
Connolly, Séamus 226
Connor, Matt 194
Conroy, Denis 47
Conway, Jerome 168, 176
Cooper, Chadwick S. 62
Cooper, Colm 'Gooch' 21, 25, 113, 114, 119, 120, 124, 215–17, 224
Corkery, Colin 106, 201
Corrigan, Colman 106
Costello, Tom 60
Courtney, Mary 187
Creedon, John 222
Cremin, Gus 156
Cronin, John 110
Crowley, Derry 67
Crowley, Din Joe 68, 192
Crowley, Jim 132
Crowley, Johnny 201
Crowley, Tadge 41, 47, 68
Cullen, Paddy 82, 112, 148, 212
Culligan, Paddy 38
Culloty, Johnny 25, 47, 57, 66, 67, 68, 70, 71, 75, 110, 158, 189–91
Cummins, Ray 106
Cunningham, Tom 37
Curley, Michael 112
Curran, Mary Jo 182–3
Curtin, Fr 42
Curtin, Sue 181

D

Dalton, Noel 38
Daly, Donal 166
Daly, Maria 175
Daly, Sharon 175
Darby, Seamus 26, 90, 109, 150, 152
Deenihan, Jimmy 19, 75, 79,

81, 86, 143, 144, 145, 148, 152, 220
Devine, Jackie 68
Devine, John 120
Devir, Brian 49
Dillon, Josephine 180
Doherty, Margaret 180, 181
Doherty, Marian 183
Doherty, Paddy 54, 70, 199
Doherty, Sean 139, 141
Donaghy, Kieran 38, 115, 116, 120, 217, 224
Donnelly, Sheila 180
Donoghue, Bernie 180, 181
Donoghue, Eileen 181, 183
Donoghue, Nora 181
Dooher, Brian 119
Dowd, Teddy 169
Dowling, Eddie 25, 157
Dowling, Jack 39, 44
Dowling, John 33, 38, 42, 191, 198, 210, 230
Doyle, Bobby 111
Doyle, Miko 37
Doyle, Tommy 146
Duggan, Gaffney 99
Dunne, John 'Tull' 55, 56
Dunne, Mick 197
Dunphy, Eamon 90
Dwyer, Dan 222

E

Earley, Dermot 226
Egan, Jerry 152
Egan, John 26, 75, 78, 80–3, 88, 110–11,112, 139, 150–3, 212, 213
Enright, Shane 116, 224
Evers, Frank 132

F

Fanning, Pat 42–3
Farrell, Dessie 112
Fay, Darren 216
Ferguson, Des 132
Ferris, Mary 181
Finnegan, Paudie 67
Finucane, Mick 25
Fitzgerald, Alan, 244
Fitzgerald, Dick 25, 60, 190, 215
Fitzgerald, John 171
Fitzgerald, Maurice 25, 112, 113, 182, 209, 210, 213–15
Fitzgerald, Mick 179–82, 185, 187
Fitzgerald, Ned 40, 41, 42
Fitzgerald, Niall 37, 106
Fitzgerald, P.P. 230
Fitzgerald, Pop 38, 42
Fitzmaurice, Eamonn 28, 94, 95, 123, 224–5
Fitzmaurice, Gabriel 188–9, 211
Flaherty, Paddy 132
Fleming, Jimmy 98
Fleming, Mick 67
Flynn, Danny 50
Flynn, Nellie 210
Fogarty, Genie 31, 32, 82
Foley, Denis 38
Foley, Jack 174
Foley, Jim 174
Foley, Jimmy 175
Foley, Mick 174
Foley, Paddy 24, 30
Freeney, Ollie 110, 132

G

Galvin, Murt 98, 99
Galvin, Paul 107, 115, 122, 217
Garrett, Mick 57
Geaney, Dave 89, 131
Geaney, Mary 179, 180, 181
Geaney, Paul 115, 124
Gilroy, Pat 114
Gleeson, Mick 25
Gorman, Tady 24, 227
Griffin, Cathal 223
Griffin, Kevin 89, 154, 223
Griffin, Michael 62
Griffin, Pat 67, 68, 154, 207–9
Griffin, Robbie 186
Guerin, Denis 54

H

Hall, Alan 220
Hanahoe, Tony 111, 142
Hannafin, Dermot 198
Harte, Mickey 27, 117–24
Hartnett, Pat 186
Hassett, Liam 157
Hassett, Mike 157
Haughey, Paddy 132
Hayes, Maurice 49, 51–2
Hayes, Seamus 42
Healy, Christy 31
Healy, Jimmy 154
Healy, Paddy 61, 162
Healy, Tim 61, 162
Heffernan, Kevin 11, 80, 108, 110, 132, 141
Hickey, David 111
Hickey, Marie 187
Higgins, Liam 66, 67, 89
Hogan, Eimear 222
Homan, Darren 112
Houlihan, Con 193, 212
Houlihan, Sarah 185
Hurley, Mixi 161

J

Jordan, Roisin 178
Joyce, Padraig 200, 201

K

Kealy, Brendan 116, 124
Keane, Barry John 114
Keane, Billy 142–3
Keane, John B. 19, 188
Keane, Tom 93
Keaney, Conal 113

Kearins, Mickey 81
Keaveney, Jimmy 111
Keeffe, Danno (footballer) 38, 230
Keeffe, Danno (shopkeeper) 31
Kelliher, Joan 180
Kelliher, Toots 106
Kelly, Connie 21
Kelly, Dolly 21
Kelly, Murt 72, 196
Kelly, Sean 163, 165
Kennedy, Paddy 25, 156
Kennedy, Tracy 178
Kennelly, Brendan 135–6
Kennelly, Colm 38, 210
Kennelly, Joanne 143
Kennelly, Noel 142–3, 148, 149
Kennelly, Nuala 146, 148, 149
Kennelly, Tadhg 143, 148–9
Kennelly, Tim 25, 83, 88, 89, 142–9
Keohane, Joe 89, 169, 192, 228
Kerins, Michael 42
Kerins, Pa 66
King, Frank 72
King, John 222
Kinnerk, Bill 229
Kissane, Denny 44

L

Landers, John Joe 'Purty' 229
Larkin, Alan 139
Lawler, Jim 63
Lawlor, Margaret 180, 181, 183
Lawlor, Pat 180
Leahy, Maurice 166
Leane, Martin 222, 223
Leen, Bridget 183–4
Leen, J.P. 175
Leen, Kelly 175
Lennon, Joe 53, 70, 72
Leydon, Seamus 56
Liston, Eoin 'Bomber' 83–5, 88, 112, 145, 213
Lombard, Mai 180, 181
Long, Denny 104–5, 106, 179
Long, Dinny 144
Long, Tom 20, 38, 42, 45, 52, 55, 59–60, 67, 137, 173, 208
Lovett, Declan 67
Lucy, Noel 46–7, 139
Lynch, Brendan 68, 70, 76, 78
Lynch, Ger 87, 150
Lynch, Paudie 78, 86, 87, 88, 139, 194–6
Lyne, Denny 65, 158
Lyne, Jackie 18, 25, 30, 42, 45, 65–6, 68, 70, 71, 128
Lyne, Jerome 210
Lyne, Jonathan 116
Lyne, Canon Mickey 65
Lyne, Tadhgie 18, 25, 30, 38, 42, 106, 110, 209–11
Lyne, Ted 65
Lyons, Tim 'Tiger' 38, 41, 42

M

Mac Gearailt, Seamus 76
Mackey, Mick 226
McAlarney, Colm 70
McAuliffe, Dan 38, 42, 133, 137
McCabe, Kevin 118
McCartan, Dan 52
McCartan, James 54
McCarthy, Denis 72, 141
McCarthy, John 111
McCarthy, Kieran 214
McCarthy, Pat 195
McCarthy, Teddy 106
McConnell, Pascal 120
McCormack, Kevin 35
McCorry, Bill 210
McCrohan, Owen 92, 220
McDermott, Peter 38, 51
McDonagh, Matilda 181
McElligott-Rusk, Brid 169–73
McEllistrim, Murty 175
McEllistrim, Roundy 175
McGee, Eugene 90
McGeeney, Kieran 216
McGuigan, Brian 119
McKeever, Jim 129
McKenna, Gerald 42, 71, 72, 73
McLoughlin, Dell 181
McMahon, Garry 25, 45, 133, 137, 138, 147
McMahon, Joe 120
McMahon, Justin 120
McManamon, Kevin, 114, 115
McSwiney, Sandy 175
Mahon, Jack 197
Mahoney, Mick 98
Mannion, Paul 115
Mason, Jenny 180
Mellon, Ryan 119
Moloney, John 140
Moloney, Matt 169
Moloney, Sue 180, 181
Moran, Collie 112
Moran, David 224
Moran, Ogie 27, 79, 204
Morgan, Billy 21, 103, 106
Moriarty, Denis 38
Moriarty, Dominic 38
Moriarty, Jackie 181
Moriarty, John 23
Moriarty, Paddy 'Whacker' 144–5
Moriarty, Tom 38, 39, 44
Moynihan, Dermie 164
Moynihan, Mickey 21, 174
Moynihan, Pat 66, 70
Moynihan, Seamus 200–2

Mulligan, Owen 119
Mullins, Brian 111, 204, 227
Mulvihill, Johnny 144
Mulvihill, Tom 68
Murphy, Brian 105, 196
Murphy, Diarmuid 113, 119
Murphy, Donie 18, 30, 210
Murphy, Eric 92
Murphy, Esther 180
Murphy, Jas 127–8
Murphy, Johnny 69–70
Murphy, Leo 52, 54
Murphy, Marie 180, 181
Murphy, Mick 38
Murphy, Paddy 134
Murphy, Padraig 198
Murphy, Paul 224
Murphy, Seamus 25, 66, 67, 130, 191–2
Murphy, Sean 25, 38, 39, 44, 110, 133, 192, 196–9
Murphy, Vinny 112
Murphy, Weeshie 47
Murray, Dan 106, 131
Mussen, Kevin 54

N

Nelligan, Charlie 204
Nessan, Rev. Fr 47
Nestor, Brendan 56

O

O'Brien, Jimmy 20, 33, 70
O'Brien, Josie 206
O'Callaghan, Bernie 55, 67, 138
Ó Cinnéide, Dara 27, 118, 119
O'Connell, Ann 181
O'Connell, Mick 25, 34, 38, 40, 42, 45, 46, 52, 53, 56, 66, 67, 70, 108, 109, 128–38, 192, 193, 195, 198, 203, 206, 208, 227
O'Connell, Patsy 'Skin' 144
O'Connell, Rosaleen 130, 135
O'Connor, Annette 181
O'Connor, Ben 158
O'Connor, Eileen 181
O'Connor, Jack 55, 89, 113, 114, 117, 120
O'Connor, Jerdie 53
O'Connor, Jerry 158
O'Connor, Mary 180
O'Connor, Seamus 215
O'Connor, T.T. 32
O'Connor, Teddy 33, 157
O'Donnell, Dom 68
O'Donoghue, Diarmuid 158
O'Donoghue, Eamon 67, 205–7
O'Donoghue, Hal 38
O'Donoghue, James 25, 96, 115, 116, 124
O'Donoghue, Paud 67, 205
O'Donoghue, Sean 44
O'Donovan, Ambrose 21, 159, 184
O'Driscoll, Gay 82
O'Driscoll, Gene 137
O'Driscoll, Ger 82, 111
O'Driscoll, Paddy 106
O'Dwyer, Mick 11, 25, 35, 40, 42, 45, 52, 53, 66, 67, 68, 71–93, 104, 110, 112, 118, 141, 145, 146, 151, 185, 194, 195, 204–5, 208, 219–20, 227, 228
O'Gara, Eoghan 115
O'Grady, Michael 68
O'Hagan, Damian 118
O'Hagan, Patsy 54
O'Keeffe, Dan see Keeffe, Danno
O'Keeffe, Frank 193
O'Keeffe, Ger 75, 86, 89–90, 92, 144
O'Keeffe, John 76, 79, 85, 86, 144, 192–5, 203, 230
O'Keeffe, Kieran 165
O'Leary, Cathal 132
O'Leary, Donal (Donie) 164, 222
O'Leary, Helen 101
O'Leary, John 176
O'Leary, Johnny 101
O'Leary, Timmy 25
O'Leary, Treasa 101
O'Loinsigh, Michael 44
O'Mahony, Aidan 224
O'Mahony, Paudie 75, 81, 82
O'Meara, Pat 44
Ó Muircheartaigh, Micheál 190
O'Neill, Donal ('Marcus') 38, 39, 40, 43, 44
O'Neill, Sean 49, 54, 69
O'Regan, Martin 'Bracker' 229
O'Reilly, Paddy 38
O'Reilly, Tadge 38
O'Riordan, Bernie 223
O'Riordan, Owen 154
Ó Ruairc, Micheál 44
Ó Sé, Beatrice 22–3
Ó Sé, Darragh 25, 118, 173, 202, 227
Ó Sé, Marc 25, 116, 173, 202–3
Ó Sé, Páidí 22, 25, 27, 75, 81, 83, 97, 99, 143, 173, 175, 194, 204, 225, 226
Ó Sé, Tomás 25, 113, 119, 173, 202, 217
O'Shea, Denis 173
O'Shea, Denny/Dinny 38, 39, 41, 42
O'Shea, Derry 25, 67
O'Shea, Eileen 180
O'Shea, Jack 25, 150, 183, 204, 205, 212
O'Shea, Jerome 25, 38, 40, 41, 42, 110, 131, 198
O'Shea, John 90

O'Shea, John 'Thorny' 67
O'Shea, Maureen 168, 173–8
O'Shea, Mort 162
O'Shea, Paddy 163
O'Shea, Pat 72, 89, 121, 163
O'Shea, Sean 74, 163
O'Shea, Seanie 163
O'Sullivan, Ann Marie 223
O'Sullivan, Annie 160–1
O'Sullivan, Fr Anthony 154
O'Sullivan, Billy 161
O'Sullivan, Con Paddy 21
O'Sullivan, Darren 113, 116, 153–6
O'Sullivan, Declan, 97, 120
O'Sullivan, Derry 154
O'Sullivan, Donie 21, 32, 67, 76, 137, 139
O'Sullivan, Eamon 176
O'Sullivan, Dr Eamonn 30, 42, 51, 57, 58, 60, 85, 134, 156, 209
O'Sullivan, Garry 221
O'Sullivan, Gerald 39, 42, 59, 60
O'Sullivan, Joe 46
O'Sullivan, Kathleen 222
O'Sullivan, Kevin Jer 106
O'Sullivan, Mattie 160
O'Sullivan, Michael 205
O'Sullivan, Michael (Mysie) 160
O, Sullivan, Mickey 'Cut'
O'Sullivan, Mickey Ned 71, 73, 77, 80, 81–2, 111, 139–42, 195
O'Sullivan, Neilly 154, 160
O'Sullivan, Peadar 154
O'Sullivan, Tom 113

P

Palmer, Micksie 45, 110, 128
Power, Ger 25, 75, 78, 82, 144, 145, 146, 194, 212
Power, Jackie 228
Prendergast, Philomena 173
Prendergast, Tom 67
Prendeville, Ashley 175
Puirséil, Padraig 199
Purcell, Sean 37–8, 199
Purdy, John 70

Q

Quill, Marion 180
Quirke, Micheál 38

R

Reen, Bernie 161–8
Reen, Birdie 162
Reen, Denis 163, 175, 177
Regan, Ann 222
Regan, Ted 222
Reynolds, Mick 57
Rintoul, Alex 179, 180
Roche, Ned 38, 42
Rode, Mark 227
Rooney, Peter 69
Russell, Mike Frank 25
Russell, Paul 210
Ryan, Eric 46
Ryan, Johnny 36

S

Saunders, John 67
Sayers, Liam 165
Sheehan, Brian 116, 223
Sheehan, Donie 72, 89, 140
Sheehy, Brian 67, 136, 169
Sheehy, Frank 44
Sheehy, John Joe 24, 42, 43, 44, 127, 136, 170, 228, 229
Sheehy, Mikey 25, 75, 76, 77, 88, 105, 111–12, 118, 144, 146, 148, 210–13, 230
Sheehy, Niall 55, 67, 136, 169
Sheehy, Paudie 25, 38, 42, 106, 136, 169, 198
Sheehy, Sean Óg 45, 66, 136–9, 169
Slattery, Helen 180, 181
Smyth, Joseph, G. 17
Spillane, Mick 86, 204
Spillane, Pat 78, 81, 82, 111, 118, 119, 141, 145, 204, 210, 213
Spring, Dan 228, 230
Stack, Austin 63
Stack, Bob 25
Stack, Stephen 144
Stockwell, Frank 37, 38, 56
Stuart, Phil 130
Sullivan, Mike 154

T

Thompson, Noreen 181
Tompkins, Larry
Twiss, Peter 167

W

Walsh, Barry 204
Walsh, Christy 38
Walsh, Donnchadh 115, 116
Walsh, Jack 25
Walsh, Johnny 25, 59, 60
Walsh, Dr Martin 50
Walsh, Mickey 66
Walsh, Sean (Moyvane) 144, 158, 176
Walsh, Seanie 105, 111, 203–5, 227
Walsh, Tommy 115, 116, 120, 228
White, Paddy 185
Whyte, George 41
Williams, Richard 180

Y

Young, Killian 116

ALSO AVAILABLE FROM
THE O'BRIEN PRESS

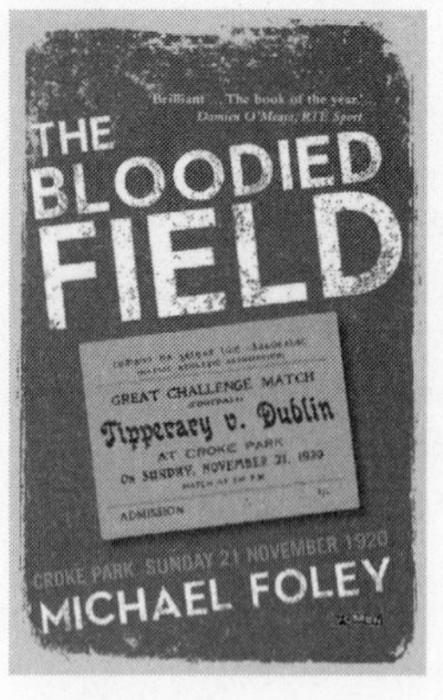

Winner of the GAA McNamee Award for Best GAA Publication. Michael Foley recounts the story of Bloody Sunday 1920 and the shooting in Croke Park that changed history forever. He tells for the first time the stories of those killed, of the police and military personnel, and of the families left shattered in the aftermath, all against the backdrop of a fierce conflict that stretched from the streets of Dublin and the hedgerows of Tipperary to the halls of Westminster.

'A sports book, a history book, a thriller . . . The best sports book of 2014.'
The Irish Times

Winner of the Boylesports Irish Sports Book of the Year. On 19 September 1982, Kerry ran out in Croke Park chasing their fifth title in a row; their Offaly opponants had dragged themselves up from their lowest ebb and now stood on the cusp of glorious reward. The outcome was an All-Ireland football final that changed lives and dramatically altered the course of football history. *Kings of September* is an epic story of triumph and loss, joy and tragedy, a story of two teams that illuminated a grim period in Irish life – and enthralled a nation.

'A beautiful book and a brilliant piece of journalism.'
The Sunday Times